# 'DELTICS'
## AT WORK

# 'DELTICS'
## AT WORK
### Allan Baker and Gavin Morrison

LONDON
IAN ALLAN LTD

## Dedication

To all those who, over the years,
kept the Deltics running

*Cover*
**A fine study of No 55.018 Ballymoss on the ECML.**
*Gavin Morrison*

*Half title:*
**An historic line up at the north end of York station on 19
March 1978 showing the development of motive power
on the ECML from 1870 to the present day. Class 55 No
55.013, The Black Watch represents the Deltic era.**
*Gavin Morrison*

*Previous page:*
**The up 'Newcastle Executive' passes non stop through
Doncaster on 8 June 1977 with No 55.014 The Duke of
Wellington's Regiment at its head** *Gavin Morrison*

*Right:*
**No 55.002 The King's Own Yorkshire Light Infantry in
immaculate external condition approaches Marsden on
the 13.05 Liverpool-York on Thursday 29 October 1981.
The locomotive would be on test prior to working a rail
tour the following Saturday — notice the enthusiasts
savouring a Deltic, in their twilight weeks on normal
passenger services.**
*Gavin Morrison*

First published 1985

ISBN 0 7110 1536 8

Published by Ian Allan Ltd, Shepperton, Surrey;
and printed by Ian Allan Printing Ltd at their works
at Coombelands in Runnymede, England

# Contents

# Foreword

## by Peter Townend

When the prototype 'Deltic' arrived on the Great Northern line, I was Shedmaster at Top Shed and I remained in the King's Cross Divisional Manager's office at Great Northern House with a variety of titles that changed periodically, but which included responsiblities for the maintenance of traction and rolling stock throughout the life of the 'Deltic' fleet.

From the 1950s and through the 'Deltic' era it was a period of continuous improvement in schedules on the East Coast main line, a necessity forced upon the managers of the day by competition following the construction of motorways. The LNER Pacifics, dating originally from 1922, played an important role in this general acceleration of services until finally displaced by the 'Deltics' and Class 47s. As long ago as 1935 it had been demonstrated that long distances could be run by the Pacifics at an average speed of 80mph, but overall times were inhibited by many speed restrictions. By the end of the 1950s much of the general improvement in running times was hidden by anything up to 20min added to the schedules for the Civil Engineer to carry out improvements to the track so that the 'Deltics', when available, could run over much of the route at their top speed of 100mph.

As a result of relatively minor changes in various features of the design of the Pacific locomotives, carried out late in their careers, there were no locomotive problems in the changeover to diesel traction; a period extended by the protracted delivery of the diesels. The Pacifics daily deputised on the intensive diesel diagrams, frequently, for example, working the 10.00 from King's Cross to Newcastle and arriving back at 22.10, having covered 536 miles in a little over 12 hours, with very little effective time on depots for servicing. As a result of this sort of working during one four-weekly period as late as 1961, it was an 'A4' Pacific that ran the highest mileage of any locomotive in the fleet, and more than any of the diesels available.

Although the 'Deltics' had many problems which affected their availability, some never being entirely overcome, after the small nucleus of staff at the three depots and Doncaster works had learned to live with them, these complex machines set new standards of running, reducing the time from King's Cross to Edinburgh substantially, maintaining 100mph for an increasingly large proportion of the distance and accumulating very high mileages over their relatively short service lives. Without the 'Deltics', or electrification, the competition could not have been challenged as the high power required and the low axle weight insisted on by the Civil Engineer was not available in any other design. Much of the credit for seeing this was due to Gerry Fiennes, then Line Manager of the Great Northern, and he had the personality to persuade the British Transport Commission to buy them. He was also determined to get the best out of the Pacifics until the 'Deltics' could take over from them.

From several points of view the 'Deltics' had the advantage over other diesel types by having two engines. For example, a locomotive could remain in service until a replacement engine was available in Doncaster works, and 'Deltics' would frequently reach their destinations with little loss of time if one engine failed en route. However, despite this advantage, the miles per casualty rate – defined as a loss of time amounting to five minutes or more – never in later years averaged much more than 16,000 to 18,000, and was frequently below 10,000, comparable to the Class 47s, but disappointing compared to some of the results achieved by the Pacifics in their prime.

My early memories with the 'Deltics' include the first test run to Doncaster reached in an overall time little different to that achieved before the war on the streamlined services, but with a bang from the locomotive when running at 98mph which frightened everyone on board. This was due to a flashover on the electrical machines and when the makers were asked – after many such incidents had occurred – how these could be avoided, they replied that the controller should be closed when the locomotive was passing over points and crossings, somewhat difficult to achieve on the track of the day! Another memory of the early days was a certain well known King's Cross driver who drove his 'A4' rather hard, who used 150 more gallons of fuel than usual on a return trip to Doncaster by using his usual driving techniques, which resulted in standing in stations for very long periods waiting for time. Riding 20 years later on a 'Deltic' on a non-stop run from Darlington to Stevenage the King's Cross driver illustrated the method necessary to maintain 100mph for long distances. He would let the speed creep up to about 102mph and then ease the controller until speed fell to about 98mph. It was necessary continually to open and ease the controller for most of the journey, rather in contrast to driving a steam locomotive which tended to be set by the driver for much longer distances.

Despite their problems, excessive fumes and noise, the 'Deltics' proved to be worthy successors to the steam locomotives which had long worked the main line north. Much of their success was due to the attention given by the maintenance staff at depots and Allan Baker was the last of the handful of depot managers at Finsbury Park who looked after them at the London end. It was only by living with the 'Deltics', getting to know their foibles and providing the standards of maintenance required that this success was achieved.

It is hard to realise that the Pacifics and 'Deltics' have now all gone from the East Coast route and with electrification now underway, the writing is on the wall for their successors, the High Speed Trains; such is the speed of progress.

*Peter Townend*
Torquay, January 1985

# Preface

When the Publisher first suggested that I put pen to paper and write about the 'Deltics' I have to admit that I viewed the prospect with trepidation. The demise of the locomotives was so recent, and so much seemed to have been written about them already that I couldn't see much new to be said. However, afer giving the idea some thought, I felt that I could add a new dimension to what had already been written, and I could certainly pay tribute to BR staff for all the fine work done over the years to keep them running. But the idea of producing the large number of illustrations required in this 'At Work' series again gave me cause for thought.

Thanks to the persistence of the Publisher, who accepted that the bulk of the book would cover mainly the period of my own involvement, I continued to ponder the prospects on my regular journeys from my home in Eastleigh to my place of work in Glasgow.

One day the answer came to me: my old friend Gavin Morrison still had a lot of Deltic photographs unused, and far better access to other collections than I. No sooner had I mentioned the project to Gavin than the scene was set and an agreement reached. Gavin's music and my words, surely we could make something of that!

Such is the origin of this book, and those readers who have seen Gavin Morrison's photography before need no introduction to his work. For my part, I have tried to show the locomotives in a different light than hitherto, whilst still outlining their general development and history, and to this end I have concentrated on the technical problems involved in keeping them running day in and day out. To achieve this I have drawn heavily on the experiences of those who were directly concerned, and I thank all who have assisted me in this. I have also tried to outline the conception of the locomotives in the first place, along with their controversial engines. Last but by no means least, I have gone to some length to describe the sound business and engineering decisions behind their withdrawal, premature as it may have seemed to many enthusiasts.

An aspect of the 'Deltic' locomotives that seems to have escaped attention in other works on the subject is the intensive diagramming that enabled them to acheive such high mileages. I have covered this at some length, not only by written explanaiton but more importantly by actually illustrating a set of diagrams. The 'Deltic' diagrams were, of course, among the very first 'cyclic' locomotive diagrams to be introduced in this country.

Just before his tragic death the late Brian Webb completed an extremely authoritative and erudite technical history of the 'Deltics'; let it be said right here and now that I have not attempted in any way to emulate that volume. *The Deltic Locomotives of British Rail* (David & Charles, 1982) will remain a standard work of reference on the class for a long time. Brian was an old and good friend of mine and I was pleased to have been able to assist him in his researches, not only for that book but others he wrote too. Rather, here will be found the history of the conception and construction of the 'Deltics' with a somewhat brief sketch of their 20 years in service, along with personal experiences, technical history, considered comment and criticism. I hope that in weaving all this together I have thrown a little new light and added something worthwhile to the fund of knowledge already available; for this has been my aim. However, I must stress that the views expressed are entirely my own.

I have not dwelt over-much on detailed performance statistics or logs, for these can be found in abundance in all the contemporary journals, no more have I much to say on the locomotives since preservation; there will be ample time for this in years to come.

I said earlier that I do not think Gavin Morrison's photography needs any introduction and both he and I are grateful for permission to use the work of others, thus giving as balanced a picture as possible. Gavin has tried hard to illustrate the class throughout its life and wherever possible with views not published before. Inevitably there are gaps, and considerably more material covering the later years, but the 'Deltics' can be seen in the pages that follow in all their triumphs and vicissitudes. Having helped Gavin over the years to secure some of the illustrations you see here, it has been enjoyable to work with him on this book.

If anybody had suggested to me just a few years ago that one day I might write a book about diesel locomotives, I would have laughed at them! But here one is and I hope it gives some enjoyment to those who read it, and fills a gap in the history of the 'Deltics'; I know that Gavin's photographs will.

In conclusion I cannot do better than dedicate this book to all those who, over the years kept the Deltics running, be they at depots, main works or in Divisional and Regional Headquarters. The locomotives built up a splendid track record second to none, but only because of the staff in all grades who ran, maintained and repaired them.

## Acknowledgements

It is always a pleasant task to sit down and write a few words thanking all who have assisted in the research connected with a project like this. Unfortunately, as ever, space is at a premimum and not everybody can be mentioend in the length that we would like; however, it is our sincere hope that everybody at least gets a mention.

First and foremost we would like to single out for special mention Peter Townend. Peter, who has kindly contributed the Foreword, was involved with the 'Deltics' for their entire service lives and has been of great assistance. Not only with the

information and recollections, but as chief proof reader and advisor too! His wise council and informed comment has been invaluable. Likewise Ray Smith, also closely involved with the fleet for much of its service with BR, has been of immense help. One of the authors spent an absorbing few hours over an 'hydraulic lunch' (Ray's words) where much reminiscence was exchanged! Several other friends and colleagues have been of great help and mention must be made of Allen Civil, Roger Hughes, Russell Wear and Ken Wightman. Roger is an Area Scientist with BR and shared his experiences and knowledge of oil sampling and analysis with us. The Deltic Preservation Society must also find a mention in these acknowledgements.

For permission to use manufacturers 'official' information and especially illustrations, we are indebted to GEC Traction Ltd and Paxman Diesels Ltd, both a part of GEC Ltd, and successors to English Electric and their constituent D. Napier & Son Ltd. When we suggested to them that they might like to see the drafts of the sections dealing with the controversial Deltic engines, with an offer to comment on any contentious points they might object to, they replied 'our view is that the "Deltic" can stand on its reputation'. And your author's view is that those words can also stand without further comment. Special thanks to E. W. Youldon Esq, Technical Publications Executive of Paxmans and old friend Mike Scott Publicity Director of GEC Traction Ltd.

All the photographers whose work is included are individually acknowledged alongside their respective illustrations, and to them all we are grateful. A special word of thanks to Robert Pritchard and the Worcester Locomotive Society, as custodians of the collection of the late Brian Webb.

Gratitude must also be expressed to British Railways, not only for access to information and records, but also for allowing one of the authors to participate in this book. M. V. Casey Esq, Director of Mechanical & Electrical Engineering at Board level, not only gave his 'official' approval to publish the book, but he also took time from his extremely busy professional life to read the proofs and make a number of helpful suggestions, as well as offering wise council. Mike Casey was one-time Chief Mechanical & Electrical Engineer of the Eastern Region, at the time when the first significant increases in 'Deltic' 'shopping' periodicity were underway; as will be seen it was an important stage in their service careers.

Last but by no means least, to wives Angela and Margaret, both of whom spent many evenings and weekends in splendid isolation, that their husbands might be locked away in darkrooms and studies! Angela even typed some of the manuscript, and has difficulty understanding one who spends all his working days running railways, only to come home and write about them; but then this is a secret known only to railwaymen! To them both, an enormous thank you.

*Allan Baker,*
*Braco, Perthshire.*
*January 1985*

# Introduction

Not another book about 'Deltics' one might ask, and not without justification. But then, perhaps no other BR diesel locomotive class has engendered such a strong enthusiast following, and this was especially so in their twilight years. There are a number of reasons that can be advanced for this: to mention but two – the 'Deltics' were a small select class of only 22, and had been the most powerful single unit diesel locomotive in the world on introduction. Indeed, with the exception of the unique *Kestrel,* which never became part of the general BR Fleet, they remained the most powerful in this country for their entire service lives; and only the recently introduced Class 58s have equalled them. In 1962 the West German firm of Krauss-Maffei delivered six 4,000bhp diesel-hydraulics to two American railroads (three each to the Southern Pacific and Denver & Rio Grande), and these took the world record from the 'Deltics'. Interestingly they were a challenge to the otherwise strong electric transmission school in the USA and, like the 'Deltics', two engines were installed in each locomotive, in their case 2,000bhp Maybachs. But compared with the 'Deltics' all up weight of only 99tons, they turned the scales at no less than 144tons; BR's Class 58 totals 130tons.

The 'Deltic' locomotives took the power classification 5, in a new system introduced for diesels; this was the highest power class and they were the only locomotives to be placed in it. To get the 3,300bhp installed power, two Napier 'Deltic' two-stroke opposed piston engines of triangular form were fitted, and these revolutionary power units, which were developed and hitherto used exclusively for marine applications, owe more in their conception and design to aero engine practice than any other field. Only by these means were the designers of the 1950s able to get anything more than around 2,500bhp in a diesel locomotive. There was some resistance to their purchase, despite reasonably successful prototype trials, but eventually the East Coast managers – for they were to operate on the East Coast main line – got what they wanted and the 22 locomotives, perhaps more than anything else, enabled the ECML to keep pace with its West Coast sister for many years, despite electrification of the latter, and until the High Speed Trains came along.

The records which the locomotives built up and successively broke in performance, availability or mileage covered were impressive by any standards, be they their steam predecessors or contemproary diesel types. However, their maintenance and repair costs were always high. This, and the obvious difficulty in running and maintaining such a small class – moreover one so totally different from others – proved their death knell. Once all the HSTs needed to operate the ECML were delivered and in service, nobody wanted the 'Deltics', or could have used them to their full potential. So, like Stirling's Singles, Ivatt's Atlantics and Gresley's Pacifics before them, they had to bow out to progress and go.

In their 20-odd years of service the 'Deltics' became a legend in their own time and very much a part of the everyday ECML scene, be it at King's Cross, Leeds, Edinburgh or speeding along anywhere between. With their distinctive exhaust note and names they were obvious candidates for special attention by the railway enthusiast fraternity. It was good to see so many saved – no less than six are preserved, which represents a little over 25% of the fleet. Is this a record of some sort one wonders? That one should be placed in the National Collection was anticipated, that five others should be saved privately was not and one cannot help but think that the preservation movement has gone a little overboard. It can only be hoped that the interest is maintained.

Despite their success, the conception of using this basic marine engine in a locomotive was not repeated (if one discounts the 10 Type 2 Bo-Bo 'Baby Deltics' that actually pre-dated their larger sisters, and used the smaller nine-cylinder version of the 'Deltic' engine). However, there were a number of schemes produced and among these was a 1,700bhp 18-cylinder engine in a standard BR Type 1 body shell, and two of the nine-cylinder engines in a hydraulic locomotive for the Western Region. Last of all a 4,600bhp locomotive was schemed out by English Electric and this would have had two 18-cylinder engines, uprated of course, and in a Class 50 body shell; the completed locomotive was reckoned to turn the scales at nothing more than 117tons. This would have been some locomotive. Alas, for whatever reasons these and other schemes came to naught and the medium-speed four-stroke engine of conventional form has prevailed for locomotive use in this country.

The 'Deltic' engine remains in production and development, and one cannot help but think that with all BR's service experience, one designed today, especially for rail traction and embodying that experience, would have a high success rate. But this is not to be, and the engine remains one for marine use. Indeed, the Royal Navy's latest minesweepers of the 'Brecon' class employ the non-magnetic version of the nine-cylinder 'Deltic' engine with considerable success. Equally, the oldest fighting vessels in the Royal Navy today, earlier minesweepers and minehunters dating from 1952, are also 'Deltic' powered.

*Right:*
A spécial train of eight vehicles in the then new BR livery of blue and white is ready to leave King's Cross on a demonstration run to Doncaster on 4 April 1966. The late Cecil J. Allen stands on the platform ready to board superbly turned out Finsbury Park Deltic No D9012 *Crepello.*
*British Railways*

*Far right:*
The canteen at Finsbury Park Depot is the scene of this occasion. The late Stan Page (centre), penultimate manager of the depot is presented, on his retirement, with a model of his favourite Deltic *Pinza,* by Divisional Maintenance Engineer David Fawcett. Also in the picture are Peter Townend, Divisional Traction Maintenance Engineer, Mrs Marjorie Page and daughter Jane. Stan was at Finsbury Park from its opening, and involved with diesel traction on the Great Northern from its inception.
*British Railways*

*Below:*
Line up at Finsbury Park on 20 May 1981. Left to right Nos 55.014 *The Duke of Wellington's Regiment,* 55.015 *Tulyar,* 55.012 *Crepello* and 55.009 *Alycidon;* three from the home stable and a foreigner. *Gavin Morrison*

# 1
# Genesis & Prototype

The London Midland & Scottish Railway was the first railway company successfully to pioneer main line diesel traction in this country, largely because of the initial effects of Harry Ivatt (CME July 1946–December 1947); nobody was very much surprised to find Oliver Bulleid (CME Southern Railway October 1937–December 1947) a close second. However, the return of a Labour government in the 1945 General Election ensured the nationalisation of our railways and, thus, it fell to the newly formed British Railways to place the prototypes into traffic.

Both protagonists chose an electrical transmission, no doubt due to the success already achieved with this method in the USA and on the diesel shunters already in service in this country, and a medium speed, four-stroke, direct acting, direct injection, compression-ignition heavy oil engine. (The term diesel, although in common usage, is incorrect – true diesel engines embody airblast injection. However, in view of the popularity of the term 'diesel' it will, henceforth, be used in this book).

In both cases the choice fell on the already proven and excellent English Electric (16SVT) 16-cylinder V-form turbo-charged engine having a cylinder bore of 10in and a stroke of 12in. Developments to this basic engine have kept it in production today, and in different forms it is fitted to BR's latest classes of locomotive, ie Class 56 and 58 (a 12-cylinder version in the latter).

The LMS and SR locomotives differed considerably in their mechanical parts, ie those forming the running gear and body. The LMS pair (Nos 10000 & 10001), relied more on English Electric's thinking, and this firm also supplied the remainder of the power equipment (for both LMS and SR designs) with two six-wheeled bogies – all wheels powered – and a body structure embracing what was to become a traditional English Electric feature, the nose end compartment. Bulleid, on the other hand, designed a massive plate frame bogie with three driven axles and a moving pony truck actually within the bogie frames. Whilst this kept down the axle load, the net result was a very low power/weight ratio, and severe restrictions on the radius of curves they could negotiate.

The SR triplets (Nos 10201–3) turned the scales in the range 132–135tons, Nos 10000/1 at 127tons 13cwt; all were heavy for the 1,600bhp (1,750bhp in Nos 10201–2 and 2,000bhp in No 10203 with the 16SVT Mk II engine) which their engines produced. Despite the fact that the nationalised railways initially decided to retain steam traction for main line use, much development and experimental work was undertaken with these prototypes, a lot of which came in extremely useful later, although it was perhaps not exploited as much as it might have been. The English Electric Type 4 production locomotive (Class 40) was a direct development of No 10203, and the Bulleid-style bogies were also used on the BR/Sulzer Type 4. The English Electric Type 3 was, to some extent, based on Nos 10000/1. Nevertheless, there were people with sufficient foresight to see that eventually the traction policy must change, possibly for eventual electrification, but more likely large scale dieselisation – at least for an interim period. Clearly too, weight would be at a premium. The higher the power-weight ratio, the more power for traction purposes. In this respect, the use of hydraulic transmission systems was an advantage, the Germans were already proving this, but English Electric had other ideas.

In December 1942 English Electric (see appendix 6) had acquired an interest in the old established firm of D. Napier & Son Ltd of Liverpool – famous the world over for its exhaust gas-driven turbo-chargers. Napiers had also acquired a name for themselves in the development of a high speed, two-stroke, water-cooled opposed-piston diesel engine which they christened 'Deltic'. This was due to the Delta configuration the engine took (Delta is a Greek letter of triangular formation, from which the delta of a river takes its name), with its three cranskshafts disposed at the points of an equilateral triangle, and the cylinders between them. Three cylinders per triangle – with opposed pistons – gave six pistons, and by mounting these triangular cylinder banks alongside each other, various sizes of engine could be produced, although normally of nine or 18 cylinders, ie 18 or 36 pistons. At the output end these three crankshafts were geared together, and the final output shaft could be arranged to rotate either faster, slower or at the same speed as the crankshafts themselves. It is, of course, obvious that an engine working on the two-stroke, as opposed to the four-stroke cycle, will give a better power/weight/size ratio, but designers and manufacturers did – and still do – tend to stay away from them in the high and medium speed ranges because of the other problems they present, particularly when running at high speed. Not least because, at an equal combustion efficiency, a two-stroke engine will develop double the power of a four-stroke exactly twice its size, by burning twice as much fuel and, in consequence, generating twice as much heat – all to be dissipated. Cooling, therefore, was a much greater problem and one could finish up with a cooling system so big as to counterbalance any saving in engine size! Generally, two-stroke engines are scavenge-blown with a mechanically driven blower – as were the 18-cylinder Deltic engines used by BR – and this absorbs horsepower, but it is essential to clean out the cylinder and help recharge it with air after every stroke. There is no separate stroke to do this as in a four-stroke. At higher speeds it becomes more and more difficult to clean the exhaust gases out of the cylinder, and recharge it with clean air in about half its piston stroke and thereby take full advantage of its capacity. Yet another problem is the need for the piston and its rings to pass over the cylinder ports each stroke, thereby

increasing the wear on all these components. In any event, of course, a two-stroke engine of a given size will wear at a greater rate than an equivalent four-stroke, because it is stressed more. This is one of the reasons why they are generally confined to slow speed applications.

The combination of the principles of high speed, two-stroke, and the opposed piston delta arrangement just described, resulted in an engine giving extremely high power for its size and weight; indeed, a world beater, albeit a very complicated and expensive piece of machinery. But there was another price to pay. Stresses and strains placed on the component parts resulted in a very high specification for materials and manufacture, consequently high in cost, with aluminium being used extensively at a time when the use of that metal was far less developed than it is now. But it gave the low weight and high tensile strength that no other material could compare with.

These engines had made a name for themselves – despite their high cost – in marine use, particularly motor torpedo boats, air sea rescue launches and the like for the Royal Navy and for which they had been developed as a result of Admiralty sponsorhip from 1946 onwards. They were available commercially from 1951. Somebody (the late Brian Webb attributes it to Lord Nelson himself, Chairman of English Electric) had the brainwave of coupling these engines to an electric generator and mounting them in a locomotive; not one engine, but two 18-cylinder engines rated at 1,650bhp (low by Napier's standards – in marine use, the T18-37K – the same engine virtually – gave 2,400bhp continuous, and no less than 3,100bhp as a short term maximum) would give a total of 3,300bhp and, it was reckoned, for a total locomotive weight of only around 100tons.

It would produce the most powerful single unit diesel locomotive in the world and, as we shall see, but for *Kestrel* the production versions remained so in this country for their entire, almost 20 years of life – some achievement!

So, as a private venture, English Electric commenced design work on a Co-Co locomotive on these principles in September 1951. The code name was 'Enterprise', later giving way to the name that their Napier engines went under – 'Deltic'. The term 'Diesel Prototype One' was also used internally by English Electric, and as abbreviated to DP1, illustrates the origin of the more familiar designation DP2. DP2 was a later development of the 16-cylinder engine from Nos 10000/1 in 1962, and rated at 2,700bhp, in a 'Deltic' bodyshell – it was the prototype of the later D400 or Class 50 locomotives.

Construction of the 'Deltic' commenced in the old Dick Kerr works at Preston in November 1951. It was at this works that Dick Kerr, one of the original 1918 constituents of English Electric, built their famous tramcars and where all English Electric locomotive work had, so far, been concentrated. Only later, with the acquisition of the established locomotive builders Vulcan Foundry and Robert Stephenson & Hawthorns, did English Electric move locomotive and other rail traction work away from Preston to Newton-le-Willows, Darlington and Newcastle.

The locomotive underframe consisted of longitudinal main members extending the full length, joined by many cross members and strong reinforcement at each bufferbeam. The whole was depressed between the bogies to form a well where the engines were mounted, thus giving greater headroom in that area. Complete plating over of the underframe was to prevent any possibility of oil leakage onto the bogies, and more especially the traction motors. Experience of diesel traction in this country has proved that this particular goal is one of the most difficult to achieve and bogie fires due to sparks from brake blocks igniting oil deposits are not

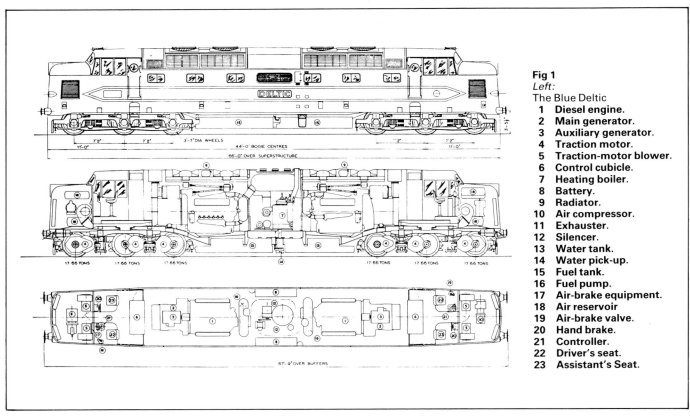

**Fig 1**
*Left:*
The Blue Deltic
1   Diesel engine.
2   Main generator.
3   Auxiliary generator.
4   Traction motor.
5   Traction-motor blower.
6   Control cubicle.
7   Heating boiler.
8   Battery.
9   Radiator.
10  Air compressor.
11  Exhauster.
12  Silencer.
13  Water tank.
14  Water pick-up.
15  Fuel tank.
16  Fuel pump.
17  Air-brake equipment.
18  Air reservoir.
19  Air-brake valve.
20  Hand brake.
21  Controller.
22  Driver's seat.
23  Assistant's Seat.

unknown. Underslung from the main frame were four fuel and two train heating boiler water tanks; the latter being on the inside. For lightness, these were all fabricated from a light alloy, and inter-connected so as to equalise levels. As might be expected for a steam railway, provision was made to pick up water from standard railway water troughs, in order to reduce the amount of water needing to be carried.

The superstructure, with the distinctive nose ends, was fabricated from rolled steel sections with much use of light alloys, especially on any removable sections, doors, louvres, roof sections etc. Indeed, great emphasis was placed on reducing weight during all design and construction stages.

The bogies broadly followed the design of Nos 10000/1, with the main load being taken by four side bearers, one at each end of each of the two bolsters, which were themselves supported by links with double-elliptical laminated springs providing suspension between bearers and bolster. From these bolsters the secondary suspension was via equalising beams underneath the axleboxes and four nests of coil springs, one nest for each beam. These are the springs that can be observed from outside and adjacent to the leading and trailing axleboxes of each bogie. The bogie frames were fabricated and riveted, the outer members being of box section.

The use of this method of load distribution ie the four side bearers, left the centre pivot to handle traction forces only, and it was thus lighter and smaller, enabling easy location of a motor on the intermediate axle. Air for cooling the motors was fed through this hollow bolster and thence via bellows to the motors themselves. The motors were six-pole dc machines which were force-ventilated, axle-hung, and nose-suspended – the axle suspension being via plain white metal bearings. Each motor was capable of producing a continuous 400bhp at 600V and 533A, driving through straight spur gearing with a 61:19 ratio. This bogie arrangement, with modifications, was extremely successful, and was also used under the production 'Deltics', the large number of Class 37s and the later Class 50 locomotives.

The main feature of the locomotive was, of course, the two 'Deltic' engines, 1,650bhp D18-25 machines running at 1,500rpm. The Admiralty had to remove pistons for ring renewal at 1,000 service hours on their 2,000bhp engines running at 2,000rpm. Clearly, this periodicity would be unacceptable for rail traction, more so with an engine of this nature when little work can be done with it in situ, particularly underneath. Thus, the derating was reckoned to give a period of at least 5,000hr between removal. Predictions at the time expressed the hope that this would increase with service experience by around 1,000hr. In the event, anything over 5,000hr with the production engines has been unusual although engines have been known to accumulate a healthy 7,000–7,500hr on occasions.

By its very nature, a two-stroke engine is a simpler mechanical machine than a four-stroke, with the lack of valves and their associated control gear. The use of the opposed piston principle gives further advantages, as in dispensing with cylinder heads it saves more weight and the resultant sealing problems, and provides efficient 'end to end' scavenging of the cylinders. This latter point is very critical with any two-stroke engine, where there is no exhaust stroke to expel the used gases, and for locomotive use a double-sided, single-stage centrifugal scavenge blower was mounted at the free end of the engine and driven by a flexible shaft from the phasing gear case; it also provided a degree of supercharging. The marine version was, more usually, turbo-charged by an exhaust gas-

driven blower as, indeed, were the nine-cylinder engines fitted to the 'Baby Deltics'.

The opposed piston principle, coupled with the triangular configuration, made an extremely rigid structure, permitting the compact disposition of cylinders with the further advantages of short engine size and low weight per horsepower. Vibration was very slight, out of balance forces negligible, and torsional stresses absolutely absent in the normal speed ranges. But the principal weight saving features were derived from the extensive use of light alloys, and only when it was essential were ferrous metals used. Obviously, such a small engine, so highly rated, needed a lot of cooling, and inhibited water was necessary to avoid erosion problems, increased in the 'Deltic' engine by the extensive use of alloys. Mounted over the top of each engine in the locomotive roof sections, were four radiators, two large ones for coolant, and two smaller ones for engine lubricating oil (which gets almost as hot as the coolant!) Twin fan units shared the cooling of these radiators, and were mechanically driven by propeller shafts from the engine phasing gear case, which was where the three crankshafts were geared together. On the prototype the flange-mounted main generator was geared to run at the same speed as the engine, ie 1,500rpm. Also from this gear case, drive was taken for the auxiliary generator, which was mounted above the main machine. It had an output of 45kW at 110V, being a four-pole machine running 1.68 times the engine speed. The extremely distinctive noise when Deltic engines are shut down and their speed dies away – usually likened to shaking a 'bag of nails' – comes from these phasing gears.

The main generators were six-pole machines fitted with six interpoles and a compensating winding, providing a continuous rating of 110kW at 1,500rpm; the maximum current being 3,000A. The main poles had twin windings, a separately excited one from the auxiliary generator and controlled via the load regulator, and the other one fed from the battery and used when the machine was being utilised as a motor for engine starting purposes, as well as providing the 'self-field'.

An obvious problem in a locomotive having two power units, is to combine the outputs of both effectively. In the 'Deltic' locomotive there were two completely separate power cubicles to house the equipment, one at each end and helping to form the bulkhead behind the respective cabs. The six motors were connected in three legs of two, each motor being in series with its mate and three legs being in parallel with each other; thus the description 'Series-Parallel'. The two generators were in series with each other and switches were provided – in the prototype they were manually operated – to enable either generator to be cut out of the circuit, thus leaving one unit to supply power to all the motors. Obviously, under these circumstances in series operation, one generator produced a lower voltage and, therefore, the power to the motors was reduced, but, of course, the locomotive's tractive effort – as opposed to horsepower – remained the same. Each unit had its own load regulator to balance engine and generator output against what the driver was calling for. Resistance was switched into and out of the main generator field coils, depending on the load required of the engine; switches within the engine governor itself initiated the load regulator action. The two engine governors were controlled by a variable supply of air pressure, depending on the position of the driver's controller.

The nose end compartments contained traction motor

blowers, one in each, a compressor in No 1 end and a vacuum exhauster in No 2. The starting battery (110V) consisting of 12 separate blocks, was located in compartments on either side of the centre of the engine room. In the square between the two engines and these battery boxes, a 2,000lb/hr capacity Vapor-Clarkson steam train heating boiler was situated.

The complete locomotive had a length of 67ft 9in over buffers, and turned the scales at 106tons in working order. The livery was a rather bright, but eye-catching light blue with yellow stripes on each body side, the name *DELTIC* in the centre, and yellow chevron stripes on the front of each nose end. Because of this she was forever known to all railwaymen as the 'Blue Deltic'.

Agreement was reached between English Electric and BR for *Deltic* to run trials and, if successful, have extended operation. Entry into service was in October 1955 after final static testing at English Electric's Netherton Works, Liverpool, and the locomotive was based at Liverpool, no doubt for ease of access by Napier personnel, the engines having been built at this works. Already it was envisaged the engines would probably prove the greatest problem.

Initial operations on freight services enabled many minor teething problems to be evaluated and corrected or modified. The first passenger turn was the 10.10 Liverpool Lime Street–Euston, and return with the down 'Shamrock', on 13 December 1955, normally an Edge Hill Class 8 Pacific diagram. Use of the ex-LMS mobile test cars enabled more scientific testing to take place on the Settle–Carlisle line in August and September the following year. During these tests a maximum tractive effect of 45,550lb was recorded with a continous horsepower at rail level of 2,650. At 40mph, 2,410hp was available at the drawbar. She was streets ahead of anything else, either available or on the drawing board.

The locomotive returned to passenger duties on the LMR until January 1959, when a transfer was effected, both to widen service experience and because of interest expressed, to the Eastern Region. First of all *Deltic* was allocated to Hornsey, and after completion, to the then new depot at Finsbury Park. In March 1961, the locomotive went to the Vulcan Foundry, its job done and a production order in hand by English Electric. It was a nice touch to save the prototype from the scrap man, and this innovative locomotive now claims a place of honour in the Science Museum, where it went in April 1963.

During its running on BR, a total of 200,000 miles was accumulated, during which time many alterations and improvements were made and many problems encountered and solved. The production locomotives benefitted considerably from the service experience gained with the prototype. Notable amongst the alterations was an increase in the locomotive's top speed of 90mph; the gear ratio was altered from 61:19 to 59:21, which raised the speed to 105mph although she was never 'officially' allowed to exceed 100mph. Alterations to the traction motor field weakening resistances gave a better characteristic during one engine operation, and thereby increase the maximum speed during these circumstances too. The 'Blue Deltic' had served her purpose well.

*Below:*
**A superb study of the Blue Deltic rushing the down Shamrock, Euston to Liverpool, past Watford Junction, believed to have been taken in the autumn of 1956. At this time the locomotive was based on Edge Hill and employed on Liverpool to London return workings. Notice that before the introduction of fixed headcodes and lights on the later production diesels, these early locomotives had to carry conventional type oil headlamps to indicate the type of train being worked.** *C.R.L. Coles*

*Above:*
**The prototype Deltic was chosen to haul a special train from Glasgow Central to Manchester on 4 December 1957, taking the Canadian Trade Mission to Lancashire after touring Scottish Industries. She is seen here in the early hours of the morning awaiting departure from Glasgow; notice the sleeping car, second behind the locomotive.**
*Brtiish Railways, Brian Webb collection*

*Right:*
**Class 5 No 44859 departs from Liverpool Lime Street as the Blue Deltic awaits its turn at the head of the up Manxman for Euston on 24 July 1958. This was a regular working for the locomotive at this time. Notice horns on the roof; conventional lamp irons; integral head and tail lamps and steam heat and vacuum train pipes.**
*Colin Boocock*

# 2
# Production Run

The prototype *Deltic* proved a number of things, not least its powers of acceleration and sustained high power compared to any other passenger locomotive on BR. However, it also proved that compared with other diesel types, ie Nos 10000/1 and 10201–3, it would be both more expensive to produce – and by a wide margin – and also more expensive to maintain, with its complex high speed engines. The engines would of course need fairly frequent removal for piston examination. It was also apparent that introduction of diesel traction on BR would be fraught with many problems and difficulties as maintenance and running staff grappled with the new steeds, so there was a strong school of thought against the 'Deltics' on these grounds alone. But there were also some people strongly in their favour.

During the period of running with the prototype, a modernisation plan, with Government backing, had been announced for BR, which spelt the death-knell of steam traction as the motive power on Britain's railways. First of all, in November 1955, it was announced that BR was to order no less than £10,000,000 worth of main line diesel locomotives as part of the major evaluation scheme. 171 locomotives of no less than 13 different types were ordered, both electrical and hydraulic transmissions were to be tried, and a number of private contractors, along with the BR workshops, were to be involved. Prolification of the 'Deltic', as already in prototype existence, was not among these orders. However, 10 Bo-Bo locomotives, employing the smaller nine-cylinder 18-piston T9-29 Napier-Deltic engine, were included. This engine, in its turbo-blown form as projected, was to be rated at 1,100bhp at 1,600rpm, placing the resulting locomotives in the Type 2 bracket of the new power classification scheme, where Type 1 was to be the lowest category. This engine was more highly stressed than its 18-cylinder sister in the 'Deltic' prototype. Electric transmission was used but thereafter the similarity between large and small 'Deltic' ends. Ubiquitously known as the 'Baby Deltics' for obvious reasons, the 10 locomotives, completed in mid-1959, had a short but nevertheless eventful life on Great Northern Suburban services. The whole fleet was a thing of the past by 1971.

Before the various pilot scheme diesels were all in traffic, let alone properly evaluated, the 1958 major railway modernisation plan was formulated and made public; it rapidly increased the orders for many of the diesel types in a plan for the complete elimination of steam traction. As events turned out, those types proposed to be increased were, by and large, the better ones. However, one or two types did get increased in numbers which, with the benefit of hindsight, would not have done so. Originally, the most powerful of the new fleet were the Derby-built 1Co-Co1 Sulzer/Crompton Parkinson Type 4s (later known as Class 44); their Sulzer 12-cylinder, four-stroke medium speed engine developing 2,300bhp. Later, this engine was uprated to give 2,500bhp (Classes 45 & 46), and eventually the Brush/Sulzer Type 4 Co-Co (Class 47) was developed, with the engine initially producing 2,750bhp. But the earlier locomotives turned the scales at 138tons, the Class 47 did a little better at around 117tons; moreover, the acute mechanical problems with the Sulzer engine uprated to 2,750bhp, eventually resulted in its general downrating to 2,580bhp. It is this figure that the whole fleet is today adjusted to deliver. The Class 47s did not start to enter service until the very end of 1962, although they had been on the way for some years. Clearly, with a maximum of 2,750bhp available at the engine output shafts, the new locomotives were going to be no world beaters. Initial units went to the Eastern Region at Finsbury Park to work alongside the 'Deltics', and completely eliminate steam from the East Coast main line.

The London Midland Region had to make do with the English Electric version of the 1Co-Co1 type, based on No 10203, and with an engine rated at 2,000bhp; the Class 40s as they later became known under the TOPS scheme were reliable, but slow and ponderous machines, turning the scales at no less than 133tons. When one appreciates what the Stanier Pacifics they replaced could daily achieve, it is little wonder that the Region's time-keeping reputation slumped. Added to which there were of course delays and other problems associated with keeping a service running with the London–Crewe main line electrification works in progress. But fewer diesels were required than steam engines, due to their considerably increased availability and consequent increased productivity of train crews, reductions in maintenance and virtual elimination of servicing staff.

However, there were some railway managers who realised early, that if BR was to stay in the long distance passenger business – InterCity as we call it today – line speeds must be increased and overall journey times reduced. The Americans were losing almost all their long distance passenger business to the airlines 'hand over fist', and despite large scale dieselisation a decade or so earlier than on BR. An average of 75mph was considered necessary in this country for the passenger business to remain viable. With the railway infrastructure as it then was, nothing running or planned would do this; except that is, the 'Deltic', with 3,300bhp under its bonnet.

In the late 1950s Gerry Fiennes was a Line Traffic Manager on the Eastern Region. Largely through the efforts of this man and his team, a case was made for a small fleet of 'Deltic' locomotives to operate a limited high-speed InterCity service on the East Coast main line. Of course then, as now, everybody realised that the real answer lay in the electrification from

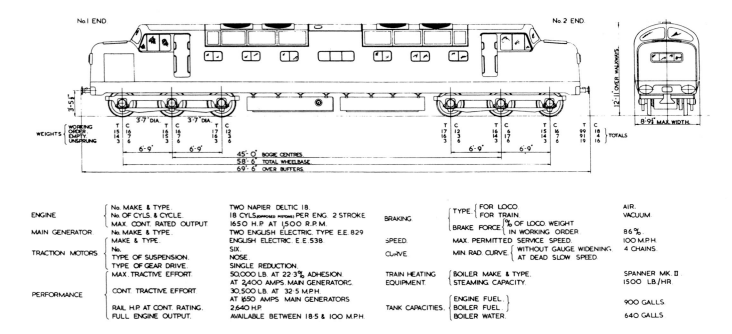

| | | | |
|---|---|---|---|
| ENGINE | No. MAKE & TYPE. / No. OF CYLS. & CYCLE. / MAX. CONT. RATED OUTPUT. | TWO NAPIER DELTIC 18. / 18 CYLS.(OPPOSED PISTONS) PER ENG. 2 STROKE / 1650 H.P. AT 1,500 R.P.M. | |
| MAIN GENERATOR | No. MAKE & TYPE. | TWO ENGLISH ELECTRIC. TYPE E.E. 829 | |
| TRACTION MOTORS | MAKE & TYPE. / No. / TYPE OF SUSPENSION. / TYPE OF GEAR DRIVE. / MAX. TRACTIVE EFFORT. | ENGLISH ELECTRIC. E.E. 538. / SIX. / NOSE. / SINGLE REDUCTION. / 50,000 LB. AT 22.3% ADHESION. AT 2,400 AMPS. MAIN GENERATORS. | |
| PERFORMANCE | CONT. TRACTIVE EFFORT. / RAIL H.P. AT CONT. RATING. / FULL ENGINE OUTPUT. | 30,500 LB. AT 32.5 M.P.H. AT 1650 AMPS MAIN GENERATORS / 2,640 H.P. / AVAILABLE BETWEEN 18.5 & 100 M.P.H. | |
| BRAKING | TYPE. FOR LOCO. / FOR TRAIN. / BRAKE FORCE. % OF LOCO. WEIGHT IN WORKING ORDER. | AIR. / VACUUM. / 86%. | |
| SPEED | MAX. PERMITTED SERVICE SPEED. | 100 M.P.H. | |
| CURVE | MIN. RAD. CURVE. WITHOUT GAUGE WIDENING AT DEAD SLOW SPEED. | 4 CHAINS. | |
| TRAIN HEATING EQUIPMENT | BOILER MAKE & TYPE. / STEAMING CAPACITY. | SPANNER MK. II / 1500 LB./HR. | |
| TANK CAPACITIES | ENGINE FUEL. / BOILER FUEL. / BOILER WATER. | 900 GALLS. / 640 GALLS. | |

King's Cross to Edinburgh, or at least Newcastle, but the necessary finance was not then available, and the LMR had beaten its East Coast rival for such money as was to be had for electrification schemes. Electrifying the ECML was deferred and, although it was appreciated that if a fleet of 'Deltics' did what was expected of them, the case for electrification would be dented, the combined Eastern, North Eastern and Scottish Regions decided to go along together in an attempt to persuade the British Transport Commission to invest in a fleet of 'Deltic' locomotives.

Despite all the arguments, eventually the case was accepted; the 23 locomotives reckoned to be needed were reduced to 22 when the order was placed. A contract was signed with the English Electric Co Ltd in May 1958; the total cost was £3,410,000 (ie £155,000 for each locomotive), and delivery of the first locomotive promised by 30 March 1960 and the last one year later to the month. Delays in delivery could

*Above and below:*
**Figures 2 & 3**
**Two views of the production 'Deltics' taken from the 'official' BR diagram book one before and one after the air brake conversion. Note the small weight differences and that in both diagrams the fuel and water capacities are shown as the same. Actually, in the later diagram they should read 826gal of fuel and 830gal of water, as this was after the removal of the water scoops.**

have saved BR over £500,000 and as events turned out these projected delivery dates were not met; however, neither did English Electric forfeit any of its contract price.

There were differences between the prototype and the production run; notable from an appearance point of view was a general clean up of the body lines to give a neater and less cluttered arrangement. Overall dimensions were reduced here and there to increase route availability, but the length over buffers was increased from 67ft 9in to 69ft 6in, and there were

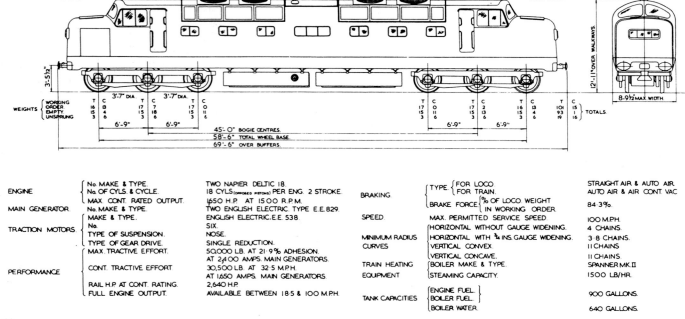

| | | | |
|---|---|---|---|
| ENGINE | No. MAKE & TYPE. / No. OF CYLS. & CYCLE. / MAX. CONT. RATED OUTPUT. | TWO NAPIER DELTIC 18. / 18 CYLS.(OPPOSED PISTONS) PER ENG. 2 STROKE. / 1650 H.P. AT 1500 R.P.M. | |
| MAIN GENERATOR | No. MAKE & TYPE. | TWO ENGLISH ELECTRIC. TYPE E.E. 829. | |
| TRACTION MOTORS | MAKE & TYPE. / No. / TYPE OF SUSPENSION. / TYPE OF GEAR DRIVE. / MAX. TRACTIVE EFFORT. | ENGLISH ELECTRIC. E.E. 538. / SIX. / NOSE. / SINGLE REDUCTION. / 50,000 LB. AT 21.9% ADHESION. AT 2,400 AMPS. MAIN GENERATORS. | |
| PERFORMANCE | CONT. TRACTIVE EFFORT. / RAIL H.P. AT CONT. RATING. / FULL ENGINE OUTPUT. | 30,500 LB. AT 32.5 M.P.H. AT 1,650 AMPS. MAIN GENERATORS. / 2,640 H.P. / AVAILABLE BETWEEN 18.5 & 100 M.P.H. | |
| BRAKING | TYPE. FOR LOCO. / FOR TRAIN. / BRAKE FORCE. % OF LOCO. WEIGHT IN WORKING ORDER. | STRAIGHT AIR & AUTO AIR. / AUTO AIR & AIR. CONT. VAC. / 84.3%. | |
| SPEED | MAX. PERMITTED SERVICE SPEED. | 100 M.P.H. | |
| MINIMUM RADIUS CURVES | HORIZONTAL WITHOUT GAUGE WIDENING. / HORIZONTAL WITH ¾ INS. GAUGE WIDENING. / VERTICAL CONVEX. / VERTICAL CONCAVE. | 4 CHAINS. / 3·8 CHAINS. / 11 CHAINS. / 11 CHAINS. | |
| TRAIN HEATING EQUIPMENT | BOILER MAKE & TYPE. / STEAMING CAPACITY. | SPANNER MK. II / 1500 LB/HR. | |
| TANK CAPACITIES | ENGINE FUEL. / BOILER FUEL. / BOILER WATER. | 900 GALLONS. / 640 GALLONS. | |

some alterations to the bogies. The prototype 'Deltic' bogie had been taken as the standard for the 1,750bhp Type 3 (later Class 37) locomotives, which began to be introduced from late 1960. However, the laminated springing of the bolsters was replaced by nests of coil springs, two nests to each bolster. The fabricated box section solebars with rivetted headstocks and cross members were retained; this was to prove a weakness later. It was this modified bogie that went under the production 'Deltic' locomotives.

The same 1,650bhp Napier D18-25 18-cylinder engines were used, but instead of being directly driven, the traction generators were geared down, the armature speed being reduced at the full engine speed of 1,500rpm, to 1,125rpm. This was an attempt to try and eliminate the generator flashover problems experienced on the prototype. The generators themselves were shorter in length, but of a larger diameter than those used on the original, being six-pole machines of English Electric type 829A, as opposed to 831A. The motors were of a slightly different type too, although of a similar rating, Type 538A instead of 526A. This new motor had four rather than six poles, thus simplifying maintenance and, theoretically, reducing the risk of flashovers. Again, both generators were connected in series across the power circuit, with the six traction motors arranged in pairs on parallel circuits. However, in the production machines, automatic arrangements were made to cut out the generator if either engine stopped, or was not available for any reason. This left the other machine to feed the complete power circuit, albeit at a reduced voltage. To assist acceleration, in such circumstances, three stages of traction motor field current diversion were provided, and these three stages automatically replaced the normal two stages, whenever an engine was not running, or a generator was not connected to the load.

The plain bearings used on the traction motor axle suspension were replaced by almost trouble-free, grease lubricated, roller bearings. The four small traction motor blowers, two in each nose end, were replaced by two, one at each end supplying air to the nearest bogie, with No 1 nose end also housing the two Reavell FRU 5.25in × 10in rotary vacuum exhausters. No 2 nose end also contained a Worthington-Simpson air compressor. All these machines were driven by individual electric motors. Each nose end also contained two $CO^2$ fire bottles, all four of which were connected to a sprinkler system throughout the engine room and nose end compartments.

A Spanner Mk II train heating boiler between the two engines replaced the Vapor-Clarkson used earlier, although English Electric as the licencees, wanted to fit the Clayton variety; such a steam generator had latterly been fitted in the prototype. Provision was made by means of a two-way water scoop, for the locomotives to take on boiler water from the conventional water troughs. The brake equipment was of Westinghouse manufacture, and the locomotives were all built at the Vulcan Foundry. As completed, all the 22 locomotives were painted in a pleasing two tone version of the BR green livery and they turned the scales at a very commendable 99 tons, less than the same makers 2,000bhp Type 4 by 34tons! They were allocated in the BR power class Type 5, the only

diesel locomotive of the time to achieve that status. All were delivered in the period March 1961–May 1962, which made them exactly one year late – it dashed the East Cost timetable planners hopes. There were numerous reasons advanced for the late delivery. English Electric blamed BR for 'messing them around' over design details and equipment specifications. BR blamed English Electric similarly, the latter claiming mitigation as they wanted to be sure BR got the best locomotive possible. In the event, it all ended reasonably amicably and BR did not evoke those clauses in the contract that would have cost the makers a penalty.

From the start, it was intended that the Locomotives would be subject to a maintenance contract, with the manufacturer remaining responsible for the quality of the maintenance and repairs beyond the guarantee period. This was originally intended to cover five years from the last delivery, and it was a completely new idea for BR to adopt.

It was largely prompted by the specialist nature of the high speed Napier 'Deltic' engines with their need for a strip down and piston overhaul at around 6,000 (projected) service hours. It was always intended that the engine would go back to Napiers works for overhaul, and eventually a float of no less than 13 spare power units (ie engine/generator sets) was built up to cover engine overhaul and repair requirements.

Basically the contract split the locomotive and its equipment into two, those parts that would be maintained by BR at its own expense, but under the supervision and to the satisfaction of English Electric, and the engines, which English Electric would undertake to maintain itself. Over and above this, only those items which one side could blame on the other, eg bad maintenance by BR staff, bad material from the makers etc, would be subject to extra costs either way. For the five-year period English Electric guaranteed that the fleet of 22 locomotives would be able, and available, to run an aggregate mileage of 4.5 million miles – almost 205,000 miles per annum per loco – except that no single locomotive would be diagrammed to exceed 220,000 miles annually. The charges reduced slightly over the contract period, starting at £700 per loco per month, and reducing to £600; there was as one would expect, a 'get-out' clause to cover variations in labour and material costs.

Inevitably, there were disagreements and arguments as to who was to pay what, and in the end it always seemed to be some lost mileage, or expensive component for which no agreement could be reached. In any event, it must have been reasonably lucrative for English Electric as the contract was renewed in 1966 for a further three years, albeit this time only covering the Napier 'Deltic' engines, and not the mileage run.

To make the maintenance contract work a platoon of field service engineers were employed, men were stationed at the depots to which the locomotives were allocated, Finsbury Park in London, Gateshead in Newcastle and Haymarket in Edinburgh and, or course, Doncaster Works. The latter was an extremely important link in the chain. Additionally, for reasons that will become apparent later, a couple of men were stationed at King's Cross station, to be readily available for any last minute problems, and to meet the locomotives on arrival at the end of each southbound trip.

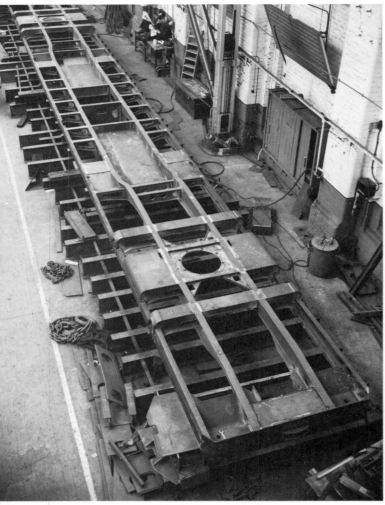

*Above left:*
**Production Deltic underframe under construction at the Vulcan Foundry and before the fitting of the top plating. The method of construction and the sunken section for the engines is clearly illustrated.** *GEC Traction Ltd, Brian Webb collection*

*Above right:*
**Another underframe in a more advanced stage of construction and** complete with the top plating. Again, the sunken wells to accommodate the engines are visible.
*GEC Traction Ltd, Brian Webb collection*

*Below:*
**Eight 'Deltics' in various stages of construction at the Vulcan Foundry. A photograph well worthy of study.**
*GEC Traction Ltd, Brian Webb collection*

*Above:*
**No D9019, on the left, in the former Robert Stephenson & Hawthorns works at Darlington for modifications and repairs under the guarantee; notice one engine is removed. At the other end of the shop can be seen Type 3s (Class 37s) under construction as well as the then English Electric standard industrial shunters along with another 'Deltic'. In the centre foreground is an inverted Type 3 underframe, and to its right are new power units and Clayton steam generators.** *GEC Traction Ltd, Brian Webb collection*

*Below left:*
**The final stage in the construction of No D9005 at Vulcan Foundry, as the body is placed on its bogies. Other Deltics are seen to the left, and in the foreground are new traction motors.**
*GEC Traction Ltd, Brian Webb collection*

*Below right:*
**A driver samples his new position, notice the twin window wipers that were to cause trouble in later years, and to the left the vacuum brake handle, replaced when the locomotives were dual braked.**
*GEC Traction Ltd, Brian Webb collection*

*Above:*
**Driver assistant's position showing handbrake wheel and controls for the water scoop.**
*GEC Traction Ltd, Brian Webb collection*

*Right:*
**A view of a 'Deltic' under construction and showing the Spanner Mk II boiler in position, but before the installation of the main engines. In the foreground can be seen the engine coolant make-up tank, and to each side of the boiler the battery compartments, above them are the engine air intakes. The combined vertical firebox and horizontal tube bank of the boiler can be seen too.**
*GEC Traction Ltd, Brian Webb collection*

*Below:*
**Two 'Deltics' returning to the Vulcan Foundry for modifications in 1961, No D9004 leads D9001, the latter by this time named *St Paddy* and being hauled by its sister. The pair are seen passing Cross Lane, Manchester.** *J.R. Carter*

# 3
# Into Service

The early years of dieselisation on the Great Northern were fraught with many misfortunes, stemming in the main from the unreliability of some of the pilot scheme diesel types introduced. These were the 'Baby Deltic' (Class 23) already referred to, and the 1,000hp North British Locomotive Co Bo-Bo diesel-electrics (Class 29). Added to the design and manufacturers' problems, the maintenance staff were unfamiliar with diesels of any type – except the shunters – and depot facilities almost non-existent. Plans had been made for a purpose-built diesel maintenance depot on the site of the old Clarence Yard coal depot, just to the south of Finsbury Park station, and on the down side of the main line. However, the construction of this would take time and, in the meantime, half of the steam shed at Hornsey had to be hurriedly partitioned and converted to house the new steeds. To enable this to be accomplished, some of the Hornsey steam allocation was transferred to King's Cross. But, and to some extent this also applied to the new depot at Finsbury Park, this was all done before anybody really knew what diesel traction maintenance was all about. There were numerous shortcomings, and the new machines had to live alongside the dirt and grime of their older stablemates. In an atmosphere of trying to convince those who had the new machines to maintain of the cleanliness needed, it was not a very auspicious beginning for the new era.

Nevertheless, all was not lost, the management was able to bring together the nucleus of a team, some of whom remained and were able to see main line diesel traction on the Great Northern into the HST era, and others who already had experience with the already proven diesel-electric shunters hitherto maintained at King's Cross, and DMUs elsewhere. Some came from places on the Region like Lincoln and Cambridge, and with the help of technical staff they gave that essential initial impetus to get things under way, learning as they went along. Fortunately, Finsbury Park depot itself, the first purpose-built main line diesel locomotive depot constructed in this country, came on-line in April 1960. Actually, some maintenance work was being done in the uncompleted building a little prior to this, but it was fully commissioned in time for the first production 'Deltics' entering service; so they, unlike the prototype, never had to suffer the consequences of being maintained alongside their steam counterparts, at least so far as the Great Northern was concerned.

Right from the very beginning it was planned to divide the fleet of 22 locomotives between the three Regions responsible for the ECML. From the eventual split, eight locomotives were allocated to Finsbury Park on the Eastern Region, six to Gateshead on the North Eastern Region and eight to Haymarket on the Scottish Region. No D9001, later just No 9001, and later still No 55.001, being the first to be delivered to

Finsbury Park in February 1961. In July of that year this locomotive was named *St Paddy,* after the racehorse that won the year's Derby and St Ledger, at that time a three-year old bay colt. It was the prelude of a policy of naming the whole fleet, the Eastern Region examples following long established ECML practice and taking the names of racehorses.

The year late delivery of the locomotives prevented any hopes of introducing the promised acceleration in the 1960 summer timetable, and continued delays frustrated the full 'Deltic' timetable for 1961 too. However, experience was gained with the new machines in the summer as they were delivered, and with around a dozen available at the time of the introduction of the winter schedules, an effort was made to accelerate certain services.

The principal problem that caused continued delays after the first examples had entered service was a series of serious fractures and associated faults in the bogie frames. Bogie bolster transom rubbing plates also came loose, followed by traction motor nose suspension bracket fractures. There were also fractures adjacent to brake hanger brackets, and breakage of transom anchor brackets. Several modifications were introduced to obviate these faults, adopted from new with the delivery of No D9005 in May 1961, and retrospectively to those already in traffic by building up a float of spare bogies already modified. As was to be expected these same problems were apparent too on the 1,750bhp Type 3 (Class 37) locomotives with the same bogie arrangement, at that time also being delivered. However, due to their generally lower speeds the failures were not quite so prevalent. Despite the various modifications problems still persisted, particularly hairline fractures in the side members of the bogies which occurred despite the headstocks being strengthened. Some locomotives even received completely new bogies of the revised design, rather than modified originals. But the fatigue fracture problems associated with these light fabricated bogies persisted, a penalty of trying to keep their weight as low as possible. Indeed, after a year or so in traffic, fractures were also discovered in the side members themselves and the headstocks continued to give trouble.

The eventual and long-term remedy was a completley new design of cast steel bogie, which was much more substantially constructed and did not use fabricated components. As a priority these new bogies went under the 'Deltics' in preference to the new Class 37 locomotives being delivered. All were fitted by late 1965. The modified plate frame bogies were repaired and used for the new Class 37 production, but otherwise all subsequent 37s had the cast variety. Nevertheless, a lot of the Class 37s retain the fabricated type to this day, and they still suffer! Incidently this is the reason why BR insisted in retaining the cast bogies from the 'Deltics' that

were sold for preservation, the whole of the bogies from the Deltics being reused under Class 37s in replacement of the worst fabricated ones.

With all these problems it was the 1962 summer service before all the fleet were able to be fully utilised, and the timetable for so long envisaged introduced. Before this could happen the timetable planners had had formidable problems interlacing these powerful new locomotives into the steam Pacific and lower powered diesel diagrams to cover the remainder of the passenger traffic, not to mention the then considerable freight still being handled on the Great Northern main line. The resultant 1962 summer diagrams are extremely interesting and were among the first true cyclic diagrams (as we know them today) introduced in this country. Without doubt they were the most intensively used locomotives in the country. In view of this, these diagrams are reproduced in full in Appendix One. Briefly however, Haymarket's eight locomotives had to cover no less than eight diagrams, with a four-day maintenance period built into one of them. This particular diagram was somewhat optimistically termed 'maintenance-stand pilot'. Thus any time not actually needed for maintenance or repair, could be put to revenue earning use. Gateshead, similarly, had six diagrams for six locomotives, with a similar maintenance period, whilst the Eastern Region handled things somewhat differently. Finsbury Park had eight diagrams for its eight locomotives, but built into the diagrams were five periods of 18hr for maintenance. This way it was claimed to be easier to get individual locomotives for maintenance, if they got out of their proper diagrams for any reason; this occurrence, as events turned out, was not infrequent! The idea of building maintenance periods into diagrams was new, and directly opposite to the normal procedure of having 'maintenance spares', ie more locomotives than diagrams to allow for successive 'stopping' of locomotives for maintenance or repair. Ironically, the latter is the more normal practice today.

Another early problem that was to plague the class – as it did most other diesel classes – was the steam heating apparatus. The rapid changeover from steam to diesel and electric traction brought with it the problem of a large fleet of passenger rolling stock equipped only for steam heating. No problem for a steam locomotive, indeed simplicity itself, but necessitating the provision of a steam boiler or generator on a diesel or electric locomotive. Despite a long-term plan to consider a complete changeover to electric heating of passenger coaches, the immediate concern was a reliable boiler or generator for the new locomotives. Right from square one it was decided that the 25kV electric locomotives on the LMR would be equipped for electric heating only, and that Region's rolling stock would be gradually changed to 'dual heat', ie steam and electric. But so far as the diesels were concerned the cost and time necessary to 'dual heat' sufficient coaches to keep up with the delivery programme was formidable. And so was started, and still persists today, a history of multi-farious problems associated with complicated, automatic oil-fired steam boilers or generators that have had to be fitted to locomotives. Let me hasten to add, that generally speaking such devices are trouble-free, as anybody with oil-fired central heating in their home or work place can testify. BR's problems stemmed from taking a reasonably reliable piece of equipment, albeit a complicated one, and using it on a constant loss system of heating, and subjecting it to all the vibration and shocks on a locomotive associated with acceleration and braking of fast trains. Not what they were

designed for at all, but all that was then available. It all compounded to make the units one of the most troublesome and unreliable single pieces of equipment of the whole modernisation programme.

There were three main types of steam heating equipment in use on BR, the American designed Clayton and Vapor, the former by this time built under licence in this country by English Electric themselves, and the latter by J. Stone of Deptford. Both these were steam generators, as opposed to boilers, and which have the water in the tubes and the heat around them. The third was the British Spanner, which employed the conventional fire tube principle. This has proved the most reliable in service, although not without its own problems; its main disadvantage was its lower steam production capacity and, in early vertical examples the long time taken to raise steam. For obvious reasons English Electric wanted to fit the Clayton to the 'Deltic' and, as we have seen, the prototype had one for a time. However, BR insisted on a boiler for which there was already proven traction experience, and they eventually selected the Spanner. Unfortunately, as events turned out, the boiler fitted proved extremely unreliable at first and of too small a capacity. It might have been better in hindsight had the locomotives had the larger capacity Clayton after all.

To obtain the steam capacity required, and to fit in the confined space, Spanners had to completely redesign their existing boilers. This is how the Spanner Mk II evolved, being a combination of vertical firebox and horizontal tube barrel, and which proved the least successful of the Spanner designs despite much modification. Apart from prototype evaluation in English Electric Type 4 No D248 during the winter of 1959–60, the production 'Deltics' were the only recipients of this boiler. It is perhaps opportune at this juncture to mention that in April 1963 'Deltic' No D9008 was fitted with an English Electric-built Clayton generator and this remained in the locomotive until May 1965. Unfortunately, or perhaps predictably, being a one-off, its reliability was below that of the Spanners after they had had some modification and the experiment was not proceeded with.

The principal problems experiencd with the Mk II Spanners were asociated with the combustion and a number of opinions were expressed, and experiments undertaken to try and achieve a better flow of combustion air and relate it to the fuel supply. Combustion problems were not helped by the position the boiler occupied in the locomotive between the two engines and with an air intake shared with them. The exhaust outlet was between the two engine exhaust outlets. Obviously, there was much interference in the air flows between the two engines and the boiler, the latter usually coming off worst. No real improvement was effected until the 'Nu-Way' burner unit originally fitted was replaced by one developed by and of Spanner manufacture – 'The Supreme' – and these started to appear from 1965. Here onwards the combustion problems diminished but never disappeared and the air-to-fuel mix remained a critical aspect of the boilers performance until the locomotives were withdrawn. The correct setting and adjustment of these burners was extremely difficult and had to be done with the locomotive operating in normal service to be sure of long term results. It was still greatly affected by air flow and turbulance around the engine air intake and exhausts and had to be finely tuned. Because of the position of the boiler between the two engines and the very noisy nature of the latter, it was no mean task to travel with the locomotives and set up the burners correctly.

Other early problems were wheelslip when starting, a penalty of high power and low weight, eventually lessened by a recalibration of the drivers controller giving him finer control. Traction motor suspension tubes suffered fracturing and also the roller bearing; manufacturers replaced these under guarantee after which no more problems were experienced with them, indicating faulty manufacture. A much more serious problem, more so in that it proved extremely difficult to completely eradicate, was electrical machine flashovers, a problem that stayed with the locomotives to the end of their lives. To the non-technically minded a flashover occurs when the insulation of the current carrying components of an electrical machine breaks down and connection is established between poles of different polarities by the current jumping or flashing between the two. The results can be imagined by anybody who has ever accidently connected the two terminals of a car battery together, only many times worse.

Flashovers can prove troublesome and sometimes extremely expensive to repair. Additionally when a traction motor or traction motors flash over, they very often cause the generator supplying them, or generators in the case of a 'Deltic', to flash over too. A large part of the problem in the early days turned out to be the high wear rate of the machine commutators and this was partly on account of the high mileages being achieved; upwards 300,000 miles per locomotive by 1964. Part of the solution was the obvious more frequent main works attention to the electrical machines and skimming of the commutators to restore their correct profile. In hindsight this should have been anticipated when the locomotive mileage was compared with seemingly less troublesome classes, but hindsight is a wonderful thing. It is difficult to describe, but very little unevenesss of a commutator surface can cause excessive bouncing of the carbon current collecting brushes and the resultant bad commutation will cause the machine to flash over. It is also difficult to detect this unevenness as it needs to be only a few thousands of an inch. So far as motors are concerned it is, of course, impossible to examine the commutation once the motor is in place under a locomotive.

Over a period, a lot of work was done by Doncaster Works on the electrical machines, both in improving their repair standards and in the depth of the repair. The control gear also came in for more attention and particular care was taken of the equipment connected with the power circuits, traction motor contactors, field divert contactors and the reversers to name but some. Later, a number of machines were completely re-wound, traction motor armatures and in some cases fields by Doncaster itself, main generator armatures at Derby. Indeed a complete refurbishment programme for the generators commenced in 1973, but because of the size and transport problems the generator carcase and fields were usually overhauled at Doncaster; some were re-wound. This was a type of work that most of the railway workshops had to grapple with as the diesel and electric fleets got older and which was never envisaged in the early days of modernisation. Some of the works built up an amazing expertise in this type of work. Indeed standards were very often higher than had previously been achieved by private contractors doing the work.

It was in connection with the traction motor flashover problem that the Deltic Service Problems Working Party really came into their own. An in-depth investigation of the problems highlighted to the representatives of the manufacturer on the committee, that over a period of years

the component parts of the English Electric Type 538 motor had been mixed up, one motor to another. This type of motor was, of course, not exclusive to the 'Deltic' being used on other locomotives too. They were also able to point out that over a period this motor had been improved considerably, and the later deliveries had a completely different type of armature winding which offered a better characteristic. Clearly if these later armatures could be combined with the best field systems, and subsequently kept together at overhaul, the performance of the motors so combined should improve. Thus a programme to achieve this was started and a better performance did result. Thereafter the polciy was to keep these better motors exclusively for the 'Deltics'. Gradually the situation regarding in-traffic flashovers improved, both by this action, a better understanding by all concerned of the repairs needed, and the generator refurbishment programme.

Having said all that it must be pointed out that the flashover problem in the dc traction equipment never completely disappeared, not only in the 'Deltic' but in other BR diesel locomotives too. To a large extent it is one of the inherent crosses the engineer has to bear with this type of electrical equipment. One opinion often voiced regarding the 'Deltic' was drivers running at too high a speed, and it is a fact that with this class of locomotive it was invariably in the high speed ranges that flashovers occurred.

Whilst on the subject of flashovers it is a good juncture, in view of what happened, to see what the Deltics were able to achieve in service. If we consult the writings of the late Cecil J. Allen describing his first production 'Deltic' experience (Trains Illustrated August 1961) we find he had been invited to be present at one of the first test runs with No D9001. The train was booked to run from King's Cross to Doncaster and back with a load of 11 vehicles grossing around 380tons and the schedule had been specially calculated to enable the locomotive to be opened out and several of the line speed restrictions had been specially relaxed for this train, and this train only. The line speed, normally 90mph had also been lifted to 100mph; it promised to be an exciting run and nobody was disappointed. The 156 miles were booked to be run in 130 minutes start-to-stop in the up direction and 126 minutes in the down. Allowing for recovery times in connection with permanent way works the net allowance in both directions was no more than an even two hours, which required an average speed from start to stop of 78mph.

Unfortunately the up journey was marred by several signal stops but on the down run the time taken was only a fraction over 125 minutes, representing a net average speed of 80mph and there were several 100s and a maximum of 102mph at Arlesey. In CJ's own words it was 'a fascinating trip and a prelude of what "Deltic" traction may be expected to give'.

What CJ did not realise was that at one point when speed was approaching 100mph the electrical machines flashed over. No one present, including the Running & Maintenance Engineer himself, the late Cyril Palmer – who was on the footplate – had ever experienced such electrical bangs before and it is no exaggeration to say that everybody was pretty frightened. However, what later became normal procedure in such circumstances: close the controller, wait a few seconds and re-apply power again, was followed and all seemed well!

It was usually in these sorts of circumstances that flashovers occurred, at high speeds and very often when the locomotive was passing over points and crossings. It was attributed to the additional vibration causing brush-bounce on the motors. This had already been mentioned in connection with worn

commutators, but equally excessive vibration of the motor which was it should be remembered, partly supported on the axle, could and did have the same effect. At one time in the early days the manufacturers seriously suggested that drivers be instructed to close the controllers when the locomotives were going over points and crossings. In those days there were of course far more places with pointwork than today, it would have been impossible to keep the schedules if drivers had to abide by this suggestion and nothing was made of it.

The damage done with a flashover had to be made good sooner or later but eventually the drivers got used to them and sometimes never even reported them. Nevertheless, I can confirm from personal experience that it is extremely frightening on the first occasion to be on a locomotive footplate when a flashover takes place, and actually being in the engine room is 10 times worse! Many were the occasions that machine covers were removed during routine scheduled maintenance to reveal that the machines had flashed over some time previously. The electricians at the depots spent hours repairing the damage, if it was very bad it might be necessary to renew a motor or send the locomotive to the main works for a replacement generator. However, by the gradual introduction of the systems already outlined in this chapter and a far better understanding by all concerned in both the causes of flashovers, how to mitigate them and improved standards both of overhaul repair and straight-forward maintenance, the problem was kept to manageable proportions.

Turning now to the engines themselves many problems arose. Initially sodium-chromate was used as a coolant inhibitor and severe cavitation of the cylinder liners resulted, paticularly around where the injector adaptors were fitted. Conventional types of coolant treatment were not suitable because of the high use of alloys in the engine; eventually the common anti-freeze solution of Ethylene-Glycol was used as being the best able to give the required protection against cavitation. In a mix 30/70 with water it remained the standard, albeit expensive treatment for the engines. Expensive because of the quantities needed to top up the system after each trip. Of course, if afforded anti-freeze properties too, a protection not given to any other BR main line diesel for many years.

It is perhaps opportune at this juncture to look at some of the major differences between the Deltic engine as used for marine purposes, and as adapted for rail traction. The original engines, later known as Series 1 and designated type D18-11B, found their way into motor torpedo boats in the Burmese, Yugoslavia, Israeli, Finnish, Japanese and German navies. Later developments introduced them to the Indian, South African and Australian navies as well as the Royal Navy. One of the major reasons for developing the Series 2 engines was to redesign the combustion chambers to obviate the then need for two fuel injectors per cylinder, as well as a reduction in machining costs with some weight saving, but nevertheless longer component life; at the same time power output increased.

The original D18-11B engine had a continuous rating of 1,875bhp, but was capable of short spurts at 2,500bhp by increasing crankshaft speed from 1,700 to 2,000rpm. The redesigned series 2T18-37K engine developed 2,400bhp and by increasing crankshaft speed from 1,800 to 2,100rpm could deliver 3,100bhp for short periods; all these engines of course, were designed for a 1,000hr strip down. The rail traction engine was a scavenge-blown – rather than turbo-blown – version of this Series 2 engine.

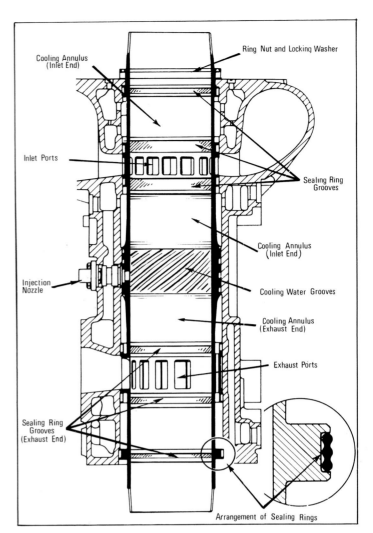

*Above:*
**Figure 4**
**The cylinder liner, notice how the inlet ports are at one end of the bore and the exhaust ports at the other; this is how the 'uniflow' principle is adopted on an opposed-piston two-stroke engine. This principle is only obtainable on a conventional two stroke by the use of ports *and* valves and it greatly assists the scavenging and re-charging of the cylinder after each stroke. This is because the cold incoming air does not have to pass over the hot exhaust ports, which would cause expansion and thus reduce the amount of air admitted. Obviously, with this arrangement the pistons have to be arranged so that the two power strokes occur together. Notice the cooling water grooves around the injector, these served not only to improve the circulation of the coolant, but equally importantly to keep the injector cool. It was in this area that most of the erosion and fracturing took place and these steel liners had chromium plated bores, being a shrink fit into the cylinder block with synthetic rubber rings to prevent coolant leakage. Axial location was via the injector adaptor and other holes that were blanked off in the case of engines, like BR's, having an electric start; in the marine version where air starting was used, they would take the air emission valves.**

The Ardleigh Type 303/1G/7 governor (manufactured by Regulateurs Europa Ltd) which incorporated a pneumatic-hydraulic actuator and load control valve, was set isochronous – that is it would return the engine to its original speed setting after a load change and it also had a 10% temporary speed droop characteristic. The governor was connected by an oil-operated servo motor to an English Electric load regulator and by these means the electrical load

on the main generator could be varied by switching resistance into and out off the generator separate field circuit.

As finally developed, the engine intended for the production locomotives was given an endurance test of something over 1,000hr and on strip down afterwards, the main problems were the Barber-Coleman spline drive assemblies. Some redesign work was necessary as well as improvements in assembly but, as we shall see, problems with these components were by no means over. Final tests of 750hr running were carried out in two engines actually installed in a locomotive and they included periods of idling, and full power acceleration and deceleration. No problems were experienced during the tests, but on strip down afterwards cylinder liner cavitation and spline wear were found. It was because of the former that coolant treatment was recommended from the entry into service of the first locomotives. The 30/70 glycol/water mixture eventually becoming standard was reckoned to restict the degree of cavitation erosion at 4,000hr to just removing the tin plating from the liners. Unfortunately, a number of engines – about 20 – had already been delivered to Vulcan Foundry for installing into locomotives before the problem with the Barber Coleman splines was realised to be as serious as it turned out to be. The phasing gearcases of all these engines had to be removed so that the necessary modifications and improvements in assembly could be effected to the drives.

Despite the problems already highlighted after testing, the spline drives – known as quill-shafts – still gave trouble in service. These shafts took the drive from the phasing gear case to the engine governor, fuel pump control shafts, over and underspeed devices, scavenge blower etc; there was trouble with fretting and the drive gear locking plates came adrift. Modified locking plates gave some improvement but quill-shaft problems remained to a lesser extent throughout the engines' life in BR service.

Retrospectively, it was obvious that the dense clouds of exhaust smoke that the Deltic engines are capable of emitting, together with the loud noise would cause complaints, especially when employed on the night-time trains. For this reason they were not used on Royal trains from an early date. There was much discussion on the smoke problem from an early date and oil carry-over depositing itself in the exhaust collector drum tanks was one of the causes. These tanks are where the three separate exhaust manifolds combine their exhaust gases into a common outlet to atmosphere. Incidently, because of the high rating of the Deltic engine and resultant high exhaust temperatures, the manifolds are cooled by the engine coolant on its way from the engine back to the radiators. In the early days problems were encountered with the tanks themselves, cracking took place around the periphery welding after around 1,000hr of running and the trouble was traced to the sub-contractor who built the tanks not having annealed the welding properly. As a temporary measure and until the tanks could be removed at Classified Repairs and rewelded correctly, additional bolts and distance pieces were fitted to relieve some of the stresses. However, after this work was complete and indeed after new tanks were made and fitted, occasional problems still occurred with the tanks and the bellows arrangement where the three exhaust pipes coupled on to them. Great care was needed in fitting the bellows or else the engine coolant could get into the manifold with catastrophic results.

Over a period of time, carbon would build up in the exhaust drum tanks from engine oil carry-over, often the result of excessive idling, and despite there being a drain-pipe it could accumulate in large quantities. These small drain-pipes were actually to allow any water to drain away if a locomotive had been left outside during periods of rain, and water had entered via the exhaust outlet. They very soon became blocked and needed to be removed and cleaned at every depot examination. Sometimes if a locomotive had been left idling for a long time the oil carry-over would catch fire when the

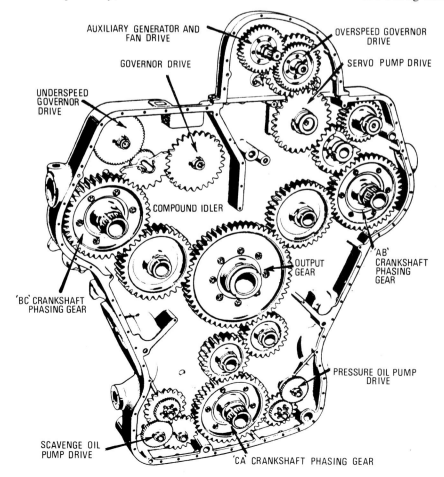

AUXILIARY GENERATOR AND FAN DRIVE

OVERSPEED GOVERNOR DRIVE

GOVERNOR DRIVE

SERVO PUMP DRIVE

UNDERSPEED GOVERNOR DRIVE

COMPOUND IDLER

'AB' CRANKSHAFT PHASING GEAR

OUTPUT GEAR

'BC' CRANKSHAFT PHASING GEAR

PRESSURE OIL PUMP DRIVE

SCAVENGE OIL PUMP DRIVE

'CA' CRANKSHAFT PHASING GEAR

*Left:*
**Figure 5**
**The phasing gearcase, this is where the three independent crankshafts were geared together, and from where the auxiliary drives were taken. Notice the double idling gears for CA crankshaft; this was on account of that crankshaft rotating the opposite way to the other two.**

27

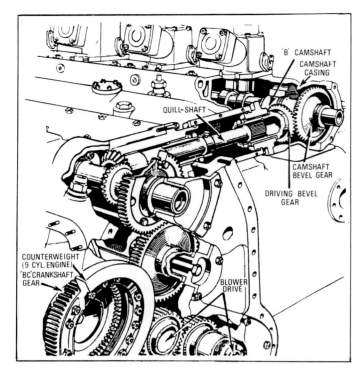

Left:
**Figure 6**

**The principle of the quill shafts, mentioned in the text, is well illustrated here. In this case the quill shaft is the one transmitting the drive from the phasing gearcase to B camshaft; notice the splined drive, this is where the fretting took place. As there were no valves on a 'Deltic', the camshaft was only necessary to drive the injector fuel pumps.**

engine was worked hard as a spark from the exhaust ignited it; in periods of dry weather this sometimes resulted in line-side fires and very often complaints were received from the fire brigades. I recall much later when the availability of the class was suffering from spare part supply problems, No 55.003 heading north after sojourning for several weeks waiting material. It was a warm summer day afer a long dry spell and she set the line-side on fire from Potters Bar to Peterborough! Taken off the train there, it was of course too late, the damage was done and by this time the carbon in the tank and the oil carry over from a cold engine had all burned away. We should have known better, and the secret was to send out such locomotives on night time trains! What had happened was that the oil already in the tank had congealed into an extremely volatile mass, and added to this would be the oil carried over on starting up; after so long a period idling, just one spark from the engine when it commenced to be worked hard and a fire would result – so will the class be remembered!

In an attempt to reduce noise levels in the driving cabs double doors were fitted between the cab and the engine room and there were partitions behind each cab seat. Eventually, added to this was a flexibale screen that could be drawn across the gap between these two partitions, so completely enclosing the crew. Despite these measures and the use of much sound insulating material in other places, noise remained a problem with the class for their entire life. Unfortunately, it was not only the crews that complained, for long and frequent were the complaints from the local residents around Finsbury Park depot which was situated in a heavily populated part of suburban north London. The regular sleeping car passengers were regular complainers too. In do not think anybody shed a tear when the locomotives ceased to work the night-time sleeping car trains.

The problems with the engines all combined to erode the intended float of spare power units to cover scheduled replacement. Napiers – to whose Liverpool works the engines were returned for repair and overhaul – were finding it difficult

and at times impossible to meet the demand. A spate of fractured cylinder lines increased the problem and led to a shortfall of repaired engines in late 1962. This caused the frequent substitution of other types of locomotives in 'Deltic' diagrams. It was fortunate that the summer was over and the use of the class less intensive, but inevitably time was lost when other locomotives had to be used in 'Deltic' timings. It was 1966 before the engine delivery rate after overhaul could cope with the demand.

As well as liner fractures, another problem which was to stay with the engines for their entire service life with BR was that of the piston – the very component that played the largest part in determining engine life anyway. Usually the separate copper crown came loose, or completely detached from the piston skirt, or body. Actually the material of the crown was 'Hidural', an alloy of copper with a small quantity – 2½% – of nickel and ½% of silicon. When the crowns came completely adrift there were usually disastrous results because the connecting rod would be free once the piston broke up, and would eventually come out through the side of the crankcase – 'putting a foot out of bed' being the colloquial and very apt phrase used. A bolted rather than a screwed and shrunk piston crown was developed, and this eliminated some of the problem, but thereafter both piston and little end gudgeon pin housing failures kept these components in the limelight, and we shall return to them again.

Below:
**Figure 7**

**Studied in conjunction with figure on page 27, this illustration shows well the multiplicity of shafts and gearwheels, and helps one to understand the complexity of the 'Deltic' engine. 1 Turbine wheel (turbo blower); 2 Turbine drive (turbo blower); 3 Blower impeller; 4 Impeller drive; 5 Blower gear trains; 6 'A' camshaft; 7 'A' camshaft; 8 'AB' flexible drive shaft; 9 Metering pump drive; 10 'BC' flexible drive shaft; 11 'AB' crankshaft gear; 12 'AB' crankshaft phasing gear; 13 'B' camshaft; 14 Compound idler; 15 Hydraulic clutch pump; 16 Governor booster pump drive; 17 Compound idler; 18 Auxiliary generator; 19 Governor drive; 20 Compound idler; 21 Tachometer drive; 22 'BC' crankshaft phasing gear; 23 'B' camshaft drive; 24 'BC' crankshaft gear; 25 Output gear; 26 'C' camshaft; 27 'C' camshaft drive; 28 Scavenge-oil pump drive; 29 'CA' crankshaft phasing gear; 30 'CA' crankshaft gear; 31 Pressure-oil pump drive; 32 'CA' flexible drive shaft.**

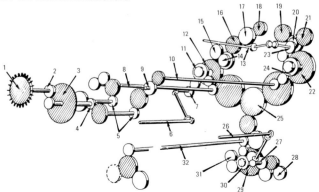

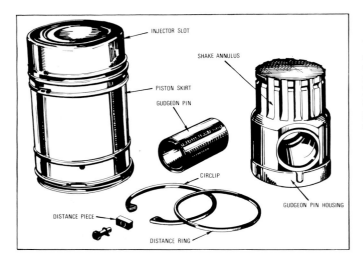

*Left:*
**Figure 8**
The original arrangement of the piston and its 'Hidural' crown and aluminium skirt and gudgeon pin housing. The crown was shrunk onto the skirt, torque loaded into position and locked through the medium of the piston ring locating pegs. Later, the crown was bolted into position. The three upper rings were the compression rings, and the three lower ones the oil scrapers, and these prevented too much oil from getting past the piston and into the combustion spaces.

Despite all these problem areas, and there were others less serious, the locomotives were doing magnificent work day in an day out. Never before had locomotives been so intensively utilised. The summer timetable for 1963 diagrammed diesel power for all the ECML services, steam being completely eliminated from King's Cross, and Top Shed closed. This final nail in the coffin of steam was made possible by the full 22 'Deltics' having been delivered and the early deliveries of the Brush-Sulzer 2,750bhp Type 4s (later Class 47) being

available. Most trains were either accelerated, had more stops inserted in their schedules, or were more heavily loaded. All the 'Deltic' main works classified overhauls were confined outside the summer period, and this gave the fleet a higher availability when they were most needed.

In the period August 1962 – after all 22 locomotives were at work – to August 1963 the fleet mileage was 3,700,000, corresponding to 160,000 engine running hours, and by the end of 1966 the fleet accumulative mileage was 19,061,000 – an average of 860,000 miles per locomotive. The diagrammed availability at this time being no less than 77%. At this rate it was not long before individual locomotives broke the million mile barrier, being the first British diesel locomotives to reach this figure.

*Above left:*
**When just one month old, No D9000 is pictured in the yard at Finsbury Park on 9 March 1961. Notice the headlamp originally fitted, and the plate frame bogies. This locomotive did not receive its name, *Royal Scots Grey* until February 1962.**
*S. Lambert*

*Left:*
**Easy work for No D9000 *St Paddy* as she passes the Wakefield locomotive shed heading the all stations 14.05 Leeds–Doncaster, this service often being used around the time of the photograph, 7 September 1961, for crew training purposes.**
*Gavin Morrison*

*Right:*

**A night scene after arrival at Kings Cross with an up express, this view of No D9002 was taken some time before April 1963 when the locomotive was named** *The King's Own Yorkshire Light Infantry.* **The water column denotes the transition from steam to diesel.** *A. A. Vickers*

*Below:*

**A fine action shot of No D9003** *Meld* **heading the up 'Flying Scotsman', but without the headboard. The train is seen here ascending the climb out of Durham to Relly Mill on 28 July 1961 and the locomotive had only received its name earlier that month. This required the removal of the British Railways symbol from the centre of the body, and its replacement with two smaller ones, one on each cab side.** *I. S. Carr*

*Above:*

**Plenty of interest in this picture of the Up Flying Scotsman, this time complete with 'Thistle' headboard and passing Tursdale Junction hauled by Haymarket's No D9004, *Queens Own Highlander,* on 10 June 1967. The tracks to the right carry the original main line of the old North Eastern Railway to Gateshead via Learnside, the more direct route on which the Deltic is travelling dates from 1872 and runs via Durham.**
*J. E. Hoggarth*

*Centre left:*

**Surrounded by Class 40s No D9005 is seen when only three months old at its home depot of Gateshead on 2 August 1961. Note the steam locomotive type shed plate, bearing the Gateshead code 52A and located under the number. This locomotive ran for nearly 2½ years before getting its name and the large British Railways symbol in the centre of the body, where the nameplates were fitted, will be noted.**
*Gavin Morrison*

*Left:*

**Two young boys admire D9006, *The Fife & Forfar Yeomanry* as she passes through York with the up Flying Scotsman.**
*Eric Treacy –*
*Millbrook House Collection*

*Above right:*
**Finsbury Park's favourite racehorse *Pinza* is seen here in original condition and before the application of the yellow warning panel, restarting the 11.00 King's Cross–Glasgow Queen Street from Berwick-on-Tweed on 24 May 1962.**
*M. Mensing*

*Right:*
**A fine night shot of No D9008 *The Green Howards* waiting to leave platform 9 at York with the 17.05 Kings Cross–Newcastle on 3 October 1964. Notice the hose pipe in the tank, as the locomotive is replenished with water for its train heating boiler.** *B. Stephenson*

*Below:*
**The North British Hotel dominates the skyline above Edinburgh Waverley station as D9009 *Alycidon* leaves with the up 'Flying Scotsman' on its 392 mile journey to London.**
*Eric Treacy –*
*Millbrook House Collection*

**Above:**
The 11.00 King's Cross–Glasgow Queen Street hurries through Hadley Wood on 31 May 1963 behind No D9010, still unnamed. In fact this locomotive ran for almost four years before being named *The Kings Own Scottish Borderer* at a ceremony at Dumfries on 8 May 1965. This locomotive, one of Haymarket's was the first 'Deltic' to accumulate two million miles in traffic. *B. Stephenson*

**Below:**
Before being named *The Royal Northumberland Fusiliers* No D9011 is seen passing Benton with the 10.50 Edinburgh–London, diverted via South Gosforth due to engineering work on 15 April 1962. This illustration is worthy of study in that the locomotive has not yet received its yellow warning panel, and for the items of ancillary interest like the old North Eastern signal post, with standard BR arms, the electrified lines and warning notices. *I. S. Carr*

*Right:*
**A classic picture at King's Cross sees D9012 *Crepello* cautiously winding her way across the complicated trackwork before starting the climb up Holloway bank towards Finsbury Park with the 09.20 express to Leeds and Bradford. On the right can be seen the locomotive depot and yard.**
*Eric Treacy –*
*Millbrook House Collection*

*Below:*
**No D9013 *The Black Watch* in rather dirty condition passes non-stop through Durham at the head of the down 'Talisman' on 2 June 1967. By this date the coaches are in the new blue & white, the locomotive still in two-tone green but with full yellow nose ends.**
*M. S. Welch*

Above:
No D9014 was only one month old when she was photographed on 29 October 1961 accelerating hard past Wennington before starting the climb to Stoke summit.
*P. H. Wells*

Left:
No D9015 *Tulyar* is just off the platform end at Sunderland as she waits to restart the 13.10 Sunday Newcastle–King's Cross train on 7 October 1962.
*I. S. Carr*

Below left:
The down 'Talisman', 16.00 King's Cross–Edinburgh, negotiates the sharp curves through Manors in the northern suburbs of Newcastle on 28 May 1962 with No D9016 in charge. *M. Mensing*

*Above:*
**The 20.20 Newcastle–King's Cross train is about to leave York on 3 October 1964 with No D9017 *The Durham Light Infantry* in charge. Notice that the locomotive still has the plate frame bogies, and the Western Region van behind the locomotive.** *B. Stephenson*

*Below:*
**In 1962 the Sunday 13.10 Newcastle–King's Cross was a regular 'Deltic' diagram and this shot shows No D9018 *Ballymoss* leaving Sunderland on 30 September 1962. Apart from this working, the only other occasions when 'Deltics' were seen at Sunderland was during diversions.** *I. S. Carr*

*Above:*
**No D9019 prior to being named bursts out of Stoke tunnel at the head of the up 'Flying Scotsman' on 21 july 1962. Notice the air horns still situated on top of the cab.**
*Gavin Morrison*

*Left:*
***Nimbus*** **No D9020 heads the up 'Heart of Midlothian' away from York with a train largely composed of the then new Mk 1 BR standard coaches**   *J. Cupit*

*Below left:*
**The up 'Queen of Scots' headed by D9021 passes non stop through the centre road at Wakefield Westgate. This 'Pullman' car train ran between Leeds and Glasgow Queen Street via Edinburgh Waverley. Notice the doors giving top access to the nose end for maintenance purposes.**
*Eric Treacy –*
*Millbrook House Collection*

*Above:*
**Mention is made in Chapter 3 of the problems associated with the dense clouds of exhaust that the 'Deltics' could emit. With only one of its engines running, No 55.022 *Royal Scots Grey* pulls empty stock out of Neville Hill carriage sidings and heads for Leeds, where they were to form the 13.50 Sunday train to King's Cross on 26 June 1977.** *Gavin Morrison*

*Below:*
**Bensham, just south of Newcastle and across the River Tyne, was a place where 'Deltics' starting their workings from that city would often cover the surrounding area with their distinctive blue fumes. Here, No 55.011 *The Royal Northumberland Fusiliers* puts on an impressive display heading the 08.30 train to King's Cross on 6 August 1977.** *Gavin Morrison*

*Above:*
One would like to caption this photoraph with photographer John Oxley's comments when the driver of No 55.019 *Royal Highland Fusilier* opened his controller at Chaloners Whin Junction! The train is the 18.10 York–King's Cross and no doubt the fumes on this occasion were due to the locomotive having stood in York station for some time prior to departure with its engines running. Because of these problems when the locomotives commenced working the King's Cross–York semi-fast trains, drivers were asked not to open the controllers fully within the York station confines.    *J. E. Oxley*

*Below:*
Beeston on the southern outskirts of Leeds was another location where fantastic exhaust effects could be observed. Here No 55.022 *Royal Scots Grey* covers the local housing estate as it heads the 10.40 Leeds–King's Cross on 3 April 1977. Notice also the exhaust lingering in the cutting near the site of the former Beeston station in the background    *Gavin Morrison*

# 4
# The Miles & The Problems

As the years went by, the 'Deltics' built up a wonderful reputation, and a number of rationalisation schemes to both track and signalling enabled a gradual speeding up of the ECML timetable, notably south of the border. So much so that by the May 1970 timetable no less than 186 miles between King's Cross and Newcastle were suitable for 95–100mph running and a number of further improvements were still in hand. Great care had to be taken by the timetable planners so that the slower Class 47-hauled trains did not interfere with those having 'Deltics' at their head. Prior to these improvements it is doubtful if the 'Deltics' needed their full power potential for more than about 25% of the time, but it was that power that gave them their amazing acceleration, and just that extra bit in hand to compensate for any out of course delays.

The spate of engine problems already outlined abated somewhat with service experience and by early 1966 the delivery of overhauled and repaired engines from Napiers was back to schedule. By the summer enough spares were available to allow a planned flow of locomotives through Doncaster Works for classified repairs. It is perhaps opportune to mention here that for the fleet of 22 locomotives needing 44 engines, a float of 13 spares were maintained. Because it was BR policy not to carry out any 'Deltic' classified repairs during the summer, to maximise availability, there was a need for some engines to be overhauled before their projected life was complete, and for others to remain in use longer. Clearly, with all the problems this did not assist Napiers repair programme at all.

In 1969 the second English Electric maintenance contract, this time covering the engines only as will be remembered, was due to expire and the decision had already been taken that henceforth, BR would undertake its own overhauls and repairs at Doncaster. The planning for this change over started in 1968 and, in fact, Doncaster had already carried out the occasional unclassified repair and some testing even before this. Nevertheless, it was a major exercise to tool up and carry out complete overhauls together with tackling any repairs, on these extremely complicated engines, so very different from the conventional diesel engines with which Doncaster was conversant. The change over was gradual, Doncaster completing its first overhaul in December 1968 and Napiers their last in mid 1969. Napiers terminated their BR production line with the overhaul of the 'nominal' 13 spare engines.

I have already outlined the overriding principle in the use of high speed, high power and low weight power units like the 'Deltic' of a short life between overhaul compared with a medium speed diesel engine. This was originally based on a projected achievement of 6,000hr. However, by this time 5,000hr was the target, and even this was rarely achieved.

Built in to any overhaul cycle must be a constant supply of spare parts and in the case of the Deltic this was out of all proportion, number for number, with any other diesel engine in use with BR. This was not only because of the more frequent overhaul periodicities, but also on account of the much finer tolerance for wear and thus a higher replacement rate. Many of the component parts in heavy medium speed diesels can be repaired over and over again, not so in an engine like the 'Deltic'. Not nearly so often could used components be re-used, and sometimes when this did happen, perhaps because of a vital supply problem, it ended in premature failure. All this contributed to a very heavy spare part requirement and, for one reason or another, problems connected with it bedeviled the Deltic locomotives throughout their service lives. Engines, and often complete locomotives were kept standing for long periods waiting for material to complete overhauls and repairs. Sometimes it was BR at fault but very often English Electric. During the years that the locomotives were in use this company went through a number of reorganisations. In November 1967, General Electric (GEC) absorbed Associated Electrical Industries (AEI), itself an amalgam of a number of smaller companies. Then in September 1968, GEC took over the English Electric Co, making the combined company one of the biggest engineering concerns in the country. Along the line lots of other smaller companies and groups had fallen into this net, and none of it went without a hitch for the customers. Napiers, so far as the Deltic engine was concerned, eventually became a part of Ruston-Paxman Diesels Ltd, itself a part of GEC Diesels Ltd, a subsidary of the parent firm. This resulted in the transfer of all Deltic engine work to the former Davey Paxman works at Colchester and it was there that all future work on the engine, and its spares, was to be concentrated. Paxman's traditional products were medium speed diesels and there was little similarity between them and the Deltic; obviously they had to go through a learning period just as Doncaster had. Difficulty with spare part supply and quality were two of the by-products of this move.

The whole situaton was clouded by the perennial piston problems, perhaps foremost of 'Deltic' engine troubles during their entire service life. The failure of a piston could be, and very often was, disastrous, with a fractured crankcase the usual result. This required expensive replacements not budgeted for in either cost or spare part stores holdings. It was and is extremely difficult to estimate years in advance spare part supply needs, and in the case of crankcases periods running into years were sometimes needed beween placing an order, and getting the finished article supplied. Large orders for expensive items like this might need Board authority first too, yet another cause of delay.

Mention must again be made of the Deltic Service Problems Working Group. This group consisted of a small number of people connected with the locomotives and they would meet regularly to discuss their problems. Similar groups existed for other types of traction and members would represent the Regions using the particular type, the maintaining workshops, the Board's Director of Mechanical & Electrical Engineering and sometimes the original manufacturers. High on the agenda of the Deltic meetings would be spare part supply problems and the representatives of the suppliers would be able to feed back to their respective companies the needs with a view to establishing priorities where necessary, and give estimates of expected deliveries. Much good work was done over the years by these groups and the results of service experience would be discussed and modifications authorised, not only for implementation by BR, but very often the manufacturers too.

It was because of the tremendous problems being experienced with the 'Deltic' engine, highlighted when Doncaster started to repair them themselves, that a sub-group was formed. The Deltic Power Unit Sub-Committee. Latterly this was very ably chaired by R. J. (Ray) Smith, who was the engineer at York Eastern Region headquarters responsible for the workshops and design aspects of diesel traction on that Region. It had soon become apparant after Doncaster took over the overhaul that the engines had rarely, if ever, achieved the 5,000hr expected of them. However, as EE rather than BR had born the repair costs, it had never really highlighted itself. BR had placed their emphasis on the number of engines available to keep locomotives in traffic, rather than individual engine life. Clearly, there was now an objective to achieve better engine life.

When the 'Deltic' engine work had been transferred by EE from Liverpool to Colchester none of the skilled artisans followed it, although several of the more senior staff did. Incidentally, it was this impending move that made EE not at all keen for BR to renew the maintenance contract; it was not just BR wanting to overhaul the engines themselves. Before the move actually took place, a number of Doncaster staff, both artisan and supervisory, were able to undergo training by Napier personnel at the Liverpool works. In an attempt to gain knowledge, some senior BR staff were also able to visit, by courtesy of the Ministry of Defence, the Royal Navy's establishment in Hampshire where the 'Deltic' engines used by the Royal Navy were overhauled. They very soon found that the Navy did not repair their engines in the accepted sense, when the engines were stripped not a single moving or wearing part was re-used in any shape or form, it was complete replacement. The cost must have been phenomenal and little was learnt from this source that would help Doncaster.

Doncaster had to learn and gain experience by the system of gradual attrition. As each successive weak part was identified and a cure successfully effected, engine life would increase until the next most stressed component would highlight itself. Cylinder liner seals were about the first that Doncaster encountered, they rotted away and allowed coolant into the combustion spaces and crankcases. It was only when this problem was eliminated by a better seal, that engine life was consistantly over the 1,000hr mark. As was perhaps to be expected the piston next came to the fore again, electrolitic action between the 'Hidural' crown and the aluminium skirt was one of the reasons why these two components, which were screwed together, came loose. As engine life was gradually increased in this way, one problem after another being

eliminated, the EE representatives on the Committee reckoned to have learnt more about the Deltic engine from BR than they ever knew themselves! Clearly, the engines had never before been used for such periods between overhauls. Doncaster built up a wonderful record and proved beyond doubt that the philosophy of downrating from the marine specification was not sufficient to achieve overhaul periodicities of the scale envisaged, much 'in-service' development was needed too.

As well as the work performed by the Committees and in the workshops and the depots, the travelling technical inspectors also developed a sense of anticipating potential engine problems. They very often stopped engines and prevented otherwise expensive damage, expensive both in terms of a failure of a locomotive out on the line and the damage done if another factured crankcase resulted. Those who have heard the near deafening noise these engines make when running,

*Below:*
**Figure 9**
**This drawing illustrates how the three independent crankshafts were phased together, and the bottom view shows clearly the disposition of the three banks of opposed pistons and their crankshafts.**

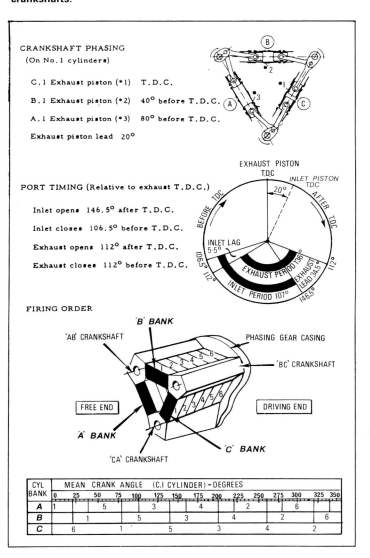

CRANKSHAFT PHASING
(On No. 1 cylinders)

C.1 Exhaust piston (*1)   T.D.C.

B.1 Exhaust piston (*2)   40° before T.D.C.

A.1 Exhaust piston (*3)   80° before T.D.C.

Exhaust piston lead   20°

PORT TIMING (Relative to exhaust T.D.C.)

Inlet opens  146.5° after T.D.C.

Inlet closes  106.5° before T.D.C.

Exhaust opens  112° after T.D.C.

Exhaust closes  112° before T.D.C.

FIRING ORDER

| CYL BANK | MEAN CRANK ANGLE (C.1 CYLINDER) -DEGREES | | | | | | | | | | | | | | |
|---|---|---|---|---|---|---|---|---|---|---|---|---|---|---|---|
| | 0 | 25 | 50 | 75 | 100 | 125 | 150 | 175 | 200 | 225 | 250 | 275 | 300 | 325 | 350 |
| A | 1 | | | 5 | | | 3 | | | 4 | | 2 | | | 6 |
| B | | 1 | | | 5 | | | 3 | | 4 | | | 2 | | | 6 |
| C | 6 | | 1 | | | 5 | | | 3 | | | 4 | | | 2 |

especially when under load, might find it difficult to understand how anybody could anticipate component failure. But the experienced could detect a slight difference in engine tone, vibration or the exhaust gas escaping from the engine crankcase breather. If the crankshafts got out of phase with one another even the non-experienced could tell!

The scavenge oil pump strainer – usually known as the 'Chip-Trap' – was another guide to potential engine failure. It would collect any particles of metal that might find their way into the engine lubricating oil system and their presence was a sure sign that an engine was in trouble. The Deltic is a dry sump engine, most diesel and petrol engines having a wet sump. In the dry sump type the reservoir of oil normally found underneath the crankcase is absent, and instead a tank of oil is located some distance away; this is necessary with a Deltic to keep the height of the engine within reasonable bounds. The scavenge oil pump draws the oil from the bottom of CA crankcase as this is where it collects, and feeds it via the strainer to the reservoir tank, it is then ready for re-circulation around the engine via another pump and filter. The strainer was examined on a regular basis during scheduled maintenance, however, it would be additionally checked for any metal particles if an engine was suspect, and many an engine had been saved extensive damage by the timely examination of this strainer revealing bits of metal from a piston or whatever.

Yet another sure guide to potential piston failure, or indeed other parts of the engine, was spectrographic examination of the lubricating oil. This is a system of analysis whereby certain metals can be detected – together with their quantities – within the oil. Clearly by this means and with regular samples excessive wear can be determined, and from the different metals discovered, the particular components wearing can be identified. For example, a high copper content – steadily increasing – would indicate a piston crown, whilst aluminium would suggest a piston body, cast iron a liner and lead a white metal bearing etc.

Oil sampling and testing had been a part of the standard maintenance procedures from the commencement of diesel traction in this country, and the depots were equipped with the relatively simple equipment needed to identify water and fuel dilution of the oil; and faults causing these can usually be comparatively easily identified and corrected. However, spectrographic analysis was introduced in the early 1960s to provide information on wear rates in engines. Clearly, it was too expensive and specialised to be installed in every depot, and it is confined to the various laboratories under the auspices of the Scientific Services Division. Briefly, the system consists of striking a high voltage electric arc between a graphite wheel rotating – and dipping – into a small dish containing the oil being sampled, and a pointed graphite electrode. The arc created excites any metallic particles in the oil film picked up by the wheel, and they emit radiations characteristic of each of the individual elements.

Many will recall from their school days the classic physics experiment of burning different substances in the flame of a bunsen burner, and noting the varying colours from the resultant flames. Each element has a different colour, and these, radiating from the metals contained in the oil being tested, pass through a small split in the spectrograph which contains a quartz prism. This reflects the light by differing quantities depending on the wave length, and thus separates the signals from the various elements. The radiation characteristics from the prism pass through exit slits placed so that each different characteristic passes through a different slit, and a photo-electric device picks up the light and measures its intensity of radiation as an electric voltage, and this is related to the quantity of whatever metal is being measured in the oil and calibrated in parts per million. Zinc, Barium, Iron, Lead, Silicon, Chromium, Aluminium, Sodium, Copper, Calcium and Phosphorus are the elements usually measured and a quantity of 100 parts per million is equivalent to approximately $1\frac{1}{3}$oz of metal per 100gal of oil.

This method has proved extremely valuable over the years in assessing general engine wear for the determination of overhaul periodicities. Once basic wear data for any particular engine is established, potential problems can be identified and, if necessary, monitored. For the bulk of the BR fleet the depot tests sufficed at the smaller 'B' examinations, a full spectrographic analysis only being called for at the larger examinations. However, the 'Deltic' got the full treatment at all 'B' exams, the original frequency of these being between 6–8 days subsequently gradually extended to 12-16 days. For both consistency and convenience all the 'Deltic' samples were analysed at the Doncaster Laboratory irrespective of where and by whom they were taken.

If an engine was suspect or being kept in service after its normal life, then special samples were taken, often as frequently as every depot visit, and despatched quickly to the laboratory where the experts were ready to provide an extremely speedy result. It was an excellent service that kept the engines in operation, and avoided expensive failures. Many was the occasion when a sample taken at either London or Edinburgh, and sent immediately by passenger train to Doncaster, resulted in a telephone call indicating that the engine from which the sample had been taken was in trouble, but the locomotive had already departed on its next trip. Quick contact with Control and the train would be stopped at a signal and the driver informed over the telephone to shut the offending engine down. If possible a replacement locomotive would be provided at some point in the journey, usually Newcastle, Doncaster or York and the one in trouble would enter works for an engine change either the same day, or the one after. These were the steps necessary to keep the fleet at maximum availability and get the last drop of work out of each engine when replacements were scarce.

Obviously, it has to be accepted that spectrographic analysis of the oil will only detect normal and excessive wear rates, it will not detect the type of failure which does not deposit metallic particles in the lubricating oil; for example fatigue cracks. However, to illustrate its effectiveness in so far as the 'Deltics' were concerned, I cannot do better than quote the figures for 1977, being one of the most critical years in the history of piston problems.

Of the 31 engines that had to be removed from locomotives before their budgeted life was complete that year, no less than eight were saved from heavy and expensive damage as a result of oil analysis. Fifteen were similarly taken out of service prematurely and saved from heavy damage following reports from technical riding inspectors, and it should be pointed out that many of these were already under observation because of earlier oil sample results. Eight engines incurred extensive damage whilst in use. The inspectors would have used 'heavy breathing' as their yardstick, indicating excessive crankcase pressure as a result of piston blow-by. When one considers the 1977 average cost of a 'Deltic' engine overhaul at £50,000, it can be seen the savings from oil analysis and riding inspectors. In the same year it was reckoned that spectrographic analysis

of lubricating oil for the whole BR fleet averaged £100 per locomotive per year; excellent value.

At the end of the day it was piston and cylinder liner problems that proved the Achilles Heel of the 'Deltic' engine in rail traction use, and it was the principal reason why anticipated engine life was never consistently achieved. The original screwed piston crowns gave way to ones that were bolted to the piston skirt as far back as 1964, around half the engines having them by early the following year. Problems persisted and an improved design of screwed crown made its apperance in late 1973; this gave an increased thread area. However, Paxmans, who were by this time doing all the Deltic engine work at Colchester, developed a better bolted crown piston and from the middle of 1974 this became standard. Unfortunately, it was to be late 1977 before it proved possible to use these in all engines because of ordering and supply hold ups. At one stage when the piston crown to skirt interface was strengthened the gudgeon pin housing was reduced in size to keep the weight of the reciprocating masses balanced; this just transferred the problem from the areas of the crown to the area of the little end, and the pistons started to fail in that area. The result, often the same – 'a leg out of bed'. The cylinder liners used to fail by fracturing in the vicinity of the injector adaptor hole. Because of the high power the cylinders developed, and in consequence heat transfer, the injectors were cooled by the engine coolant. The adaptor that bridged the gap between cylinder liner and cylinder block, and into which the injector itself fitted, was troublesome. Extreme care was necessary in fitting these adaptors and when injectors were being removed or replaced, great care had to be taken to try not to disturb them. This led to a policy of trying to keep all injector replacement as a Doncaster Works task, not because the depots were considered incompetent to perform the job without disturbing the adaptor, but because it was such a difficult task to perform with the engine in situ in a locomotive. This goal was never fully achieved, in the main because as engine life was increased when other problems were eradicated, injector renewal became due between works visits. If the adaptors were disturbed then very often the engine would fill up with coolant as it leaked by them and into the cylinders. The whole engine would then have to be drained whilst the adaptor was refitted correctly. Usually the symptom of a fractured liner or a leaking adaptor in service, was aeration of the coolant caused by combustion gasses getting into the coolant system and forcing the water out.

Fretting of the liner glands between themselves and the cylinder block was another source of concern, but the use of a coolant inhibitor greatly reduced the cavitation problem. Originally sodium-chromate was used as an additive to the water, but later the much more effective ethylene-glycol. An early re-design of the liners helped considerably, it gave more strength in the known weak points and thus reduced stresses, especially in the vicinity of the injector adaptor hole. The room available for the adaptor was increased at the same time and this allowed far more flexibility in the design of that component. Numerous types of sealing were tried over the years to prevent fracturing around the adaptor, including at one time a gold-plated adaptor; this proved an expensive failure. In the end a proprietary brand of sealant provided the answer to the electrolitic action that was taking place in the liner-adaptor interface, but it took a lot of finding.

The various engine protection devices were often the cause of unnecessary failure by malfunctions. All the systems in use had been approved by BR despite being almost exactly the same as to be found on the marine version of the 'Deltic' engine. However, in some cases approval had only been given because the locomotive was a two-engined machine and would be able to keep going even if one engine shut down. The devices fitted were:

A  Low oil pressure engine shut down
B  High engine oil temperature warning light
C  High engine coolant temperature warning light
D  Low engine coolant level shut down
E  Engine overspeed shut down
F  Engine underspeed detection – this removed the load from an engine that was running too slow
G  Coolant flow detection – this shut the engine down if their was insufficient flow.

Of these the engine overspeed and coolant flow systems were the most troublesome. As the engine had no conventional camshafts to drive the valve gear and fuel pumps, and on to which a 'normal' type overspeed device could also be fitted, it was necessary to use an 'Iso Speedric' centrifugal overspeed switch which was driven by a quill shaft from the main phasing gearcase. This responded to engine speed and should this rise to between 1,670 and 1,710rpm it would trip, and operate a 'Martonair' mechanical overspeed trip mechanism. This was a spring loaded trip arrangement which, when released by the speed sensing device, would close the three fuel pump control racks against the engine governor. The latch machanisms were delicate on both devices and the relationship between the two critical. More often than not engine overspeed shutdowns in service were the result of malfunctions by these components rather than genuine overspeeding. It was sometimes difficult to establish which of the two mechanisms had operated, the speed sensing switch or the 'Martonair' cylinder because the driver could reset the latter with a fixed reset handle, and resetting the 'Martonair' automatically reset the 'Iso Speedric' governor too. Unless the driver, or whoever else reset the mechanism, noted if the speed sensing governor had tripped, maintenance staff could easily take the wrong path. Usually it was a worn trip latch on the 'Martonair' that caused the fault and despite some redesign of this in the early days, great care was always needed if either or both components were renewed to ensure the correct relationship between them.

Coolant flow and level switches were a cause of malfunction throughout the lives of the locomotives, the former was an unusual device and the 'Deltic' was about the only BR diesel locomotive to have them. They were considered necessary by Napiers to prevent engine seizure in view of the rapid temperature rise that could take place in such a highly rated engine if the flow of coolant diminished, and before 'boiling' took place with resultant shut down with a low coolant level. Many an otherwise serviceable engine was shut down because of faults with these delicate protection switches, often the result of pitting of the electrical contact tips. Several different designs were tried over the years. It is perhaps opportune to mention here that the 'Deltic' had an arrangement whereby the engine header tanks could be topped up, even whilst the locomotive was en route, from a 'make-up' tank situated at floor level. A single semi-rotary hand pump could, by operation of a three way valve, be adjusted to deliver coolant from the 'make-up' tank to whichever engine header tank needed it. Over the years lots of failures were prevented, or delays minimised by judicious use of this pump!

The underspeed switch, which was a similar 'Iso Speedric'

speed sensing governor to the overspeed and also driven from a quill shaft off the phasing gearcase, was designed to take the electrical load off an engine if it was running too slow. This usually happened when the driver first applied power when moving a train way from rest and, like the overspeed its setting was critial. It would operate in the range 530–560rpm. As well as removing the load, it would return the engine to its normal idling speed. Considered by BR to be somewhat superfluous, and like its overspeed sister subject to malfunctions, it was removed soon after the maintenance was transferred to Doncaster, the modification being carried out by both workshops and depots.

Despite the problems, not all of which were confined to the engines as we shall see later, the locomotives continued generally to perform well and enable the ECML to remain well in the forefront of BR's diesel motive power achievements, and compete well with its electrified West Coast sister. In January 1973 history was made by a British diesel locomotive when Haymarket's No D9010, *The King's Own Scottish Borderer* clocked up no less than 2,000,000 revenue earning miles after just 12 years service. By this time seven of the regular day-time trains between King's Cross and Edinburgh completed their runs in less than six hours and with 'Deltic' haulage.

Towards the end of the 1960s, as steam was finally phased out of service, it was at last decided to embark on a programme for the replacement of steam heating on passenger trains by electricity. Despite the first 20 Class 47s (originally numbered D1500–1519 and later 47.401–47.420) having this facility from new, the majority of their later sisters did not. It was a large and costly programme and one still not complete. As well as the Class 47s already mentioned, the Class 33s and the Class

*Below:*

**Figure 10**

**Section through the cylinders viewed from the driving end. This illustrates well the symetrical triangular (Delta) formation. 1 'AB' crankshaft (9 cylinder engines); 2 'AB' crankcase; 3 Exhaust piston; 4 Coolant restrictor and liner locating plug; 5 Inlet piston; 6 'BC' crankcase; 7 'BC' crankshaft (9 cylinder engines); 8 Connecting rod; 9 Crankcase tie-bolt; 10 Drain oil manifold; 11 Exhaust manifolds; 12 'C' camshaft casing; 13 Fuel injection pump; 14 Air inlet duets; 15 Engine mounting attachment face; 16 'CA' crankcase; 17 'CA' crankshaft; 18 'CA' flexible drive shaft; 19 Castellated ring nut; 20 Cylinder liner; 21 'A' cylinder block; 22 Blower flexible drive shaft.**

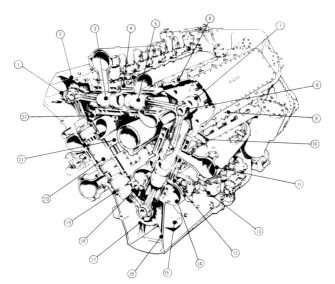

50s could also supply electric train heat, in all cases from a separate direct current (dc) generator. Subsequent conversions of Class 47, as well as conversion of Classes 31 and 45, have used alternators which supply alternating current (ac) to provide both electric train heating (ETH) and auxiliary locomotive supplies; in all cases rectification to dc is undertaken by solid state semi-conductors. The alternator provides a far more compact arrangement in the already cramped locomotive machinery compartments.

When it came to the 'Deltics', obvious early candidates for conversion, then the space problems magnified considerably with two of almost everything. Indeed, for space reasons the auxiliary generators were mounted on top of the main machines, instead of being overhung as was the practice in other diesel types; they were driven by gears from the main phasing gearcase. Thus, the use of an alternator to provide ETH and also replace the auxiliary generator was not so easy and the reluctant decision had to be taken to supply ETH direct from the main generator. This was a far from ideal situation as the main generator voltage varies depending on the power the driver requires for traction purposes, whereas a separate ETH or auxiliary machine can be regulated to deliver a constant voltage.

The whole situation was made additionally difficult as it was essential that the locomotives retained their steam heating boilers, so no space became available from their removal. As events turned out the 'Deltics' were to require their steam heating equipment for the remainder of their service lives as at that time there were no plans to either replace the Mk 1 steam heated sleeping car fleet with newer vehicles, or dual-heat them. Most of the Mk 1s completed their lives as steam heated only, and the Mk 3 sleeping car vehicles only started to come into service as the 'Deltics' were withdrawn.

One of the concepts of the East Coast timetable so far as locomotive utilisation was concerned, was that locomotives used on the day-time trains, after servicing in either London or Edinburgh in the late evening, would be able to take up duty on the night trains and vice versa. Therefore, with the introduction of ETH on the day-time trains the locomotives had to be equipped to provide either electric or steam heating.

Janaury 1967 saw the experimental provision on No D9007 of ETH taken from one of its main generators and the regional authorities and engineers alike were well pleased when the locomotive proved capable of maintaining existing schedules, despite the 350-odd bhp it was reckoned would be needed to heat and air condition the trains. Of course, the actual electrical load at any one time depends on the number of vehicles being heated, their individual machinery loadings and the ambient temperature. As converted No D9007 could only supply ETH from its No 1 main generator, but as later applied as a fleet modification either generator could supply the load and they were so arranged that the generator at the end of the locomotive from which it was being driven provided the ETH. Obviously, therefore, if the leading engine was not running for any reason, then its mate would take over ETH supply. There was one problem with the arrangement because when a train was being started the traction voltage requirement was below the minimum acceptable for ETH supply. Thus it was necessary for the ETH to be automatically switched off under these circumstances and remain so until traction voltage exceeded 600V. When the driver opened his power handle there was a small delay before power was applied, this allowed the ETH contactors to drop out if the ETH had been switched on; they would close again automatically as voltage rose. It

was not the perfect arrangement engineers and operators alike wanted, but it was an ingenious, and as events turned out, acceptable answer to the problem of taking ETH supply from the main traction generators.

Anyone who has ever caught a 'Deltic' hauled train of modern stock might have noticed the sound of the run-down of the motor alternator set on the coaches as the train started away, only to start again a few moments later – to the knowledgeable this was the tell-tale of Class 55 haulage. For this reason drivers were instructed not to run with very small controller openings for long periods, it being necessary either to close the controller completely, or keep it at least 25% open to ensure uninterrupted ETH supply. Nos D9009 and D9021 were fitted with the modified system in September and October 1970, and the whole fleet was completed by late 1971. No D9007 was the last, being brought into line with its sisters when outshopped from Doncaster after classified repairs in November 1971.

Another fleet modification was needed to enable the locomotives to work the air-braked rolling stock beginning to be introduced. The decision had been made in the mid-1960s to change over from the use of the automatic vacuum brake as a standard in this country, to the automatic air brake and this is yet another scheme still not complete. In the interim many locomotives have had to be equipped to operate braking systems of both types and this makes them extemely complicated in so far as their brake equipment is concerned. Obviously, the 'Deltics' already had equipment to operate their own air brakes, but the possibility of having an air-braked train behind them increased the requirement for compressed air and two compressors rather than one became essential. No D9016 was the first locomotive converted in October 1967, followed by No D9007, and new Davies & Metcalfe compressors were installed in No 2 nose-end replacing the Westinghouse machine; otherwise it was a Westinghouse brake system that was adopted.

The programme to equip the ECML with the new Mk 2 air-braked coaches was a rapid one and it necessitated a quick conversion of the 'Deltics' to match, remembering that many of the Class 47s were dual-braked from new. Thus, by July 1968 all 22 locomotives were converted, No D9011 being the last. It was this dual braking programme that resulted in the only substantial re-allocation of the fleet in pre-HST days and this was deemed necessary to concentrate on Finsbury Park the dual-braked locomotives as the new coaches went into that depot's diagrams first. Nos D9000, D9016 and D9019 came south from Haymarket in exchange for Nos D9001, D9003 and D9009, as the locomotives were converted during their scheduled classified repairs. All had returned 'home' on completion of the conversion programme in June 1968.

Another legacy of steam disappeared in a January 1968 decision to remove the water troughs from the ECML, the last such troughs in use in this country. This was not only because of the introduction of so many ETH trains, but also a requirement of the Civil Engineer to lift line speeds by general track improvements otherwise hampered by the presence of the troughs and all their associated problems. However, as there was still a requirement for a 'Deltic' to make a King's Cross–Newcastle non-stop run with the steam heated night trains, the capacity of their boiler water tanks had to be increased. This was achieved by using that space formally occupied by the scoop itself, and a decrease in fuel capacity of a little over 100gal. The fuel capacity went down from 940 to 826gal and the water capacity was increased from 640 to 830gal. As the locomotives were never normally diagrammed for more than one King's Cross–Edinburgh or return run, or a King's Cross–Leeds return without visiting a fuelling point, this reduction in fuel capacity was not a problem.

In an effort to increase the utilisation of the fleet to even higher levels, from the Summer timetable of 1970 they were diagrammed on an all-line basis irrespective of 'home' depot or owning Region. Control of the entire fleet was by York Regional Control and this system was to remain in force until the introduction of the HSTs. Included in the first all-line diagrams was a particular case where a single locomotive was diagrammed for no less than five trips along the entire ECML in 48 hours – about 2,000 miles – it was some diagramming even by the high standards already set by the class. But it soon became extremely rare for indiviudal locomotives to remain in the correct diagrams for very long and because of this they were altered to cover shorter 24hr periods, and even these often got shortened in practice. But the concept of overall control from York proved very effective in ensuring each diagrammed 'Deltic'-hauled train was in fact 'Deltic'-hauled.

*Below:*
**No 55.001 *St Paddy* catches the late afternoon sun as she pulls out of York on the 10.30 Aberdeen–King's Cross and passes underneath Holgate Bridge at the south end of the station on 23 September 1976.** *P. D. Hawkins*

*Left:*
**No 55.002** *The King's Own Yorkshire Light Infantry* **races towards Black Carr Junction, south of Doncaster with the 11.25 King's Cross—Leeds, just as an up freight takes the Lincoln line headed by an out of sight Class 40 on 5 February 1977.** *Gavin Morrison*

*Below left:*
**The 90mph speed restriction marker which was then at the entrance to Stoke tunnel has probably caused the driver of No 55.003** *Meld* **to ease his throttle back slightly. The train is the 15.00 King's Cross—Aberdeen on 27 May 1978.** *Gavin Morrison*

*Below:*
**After working empty stock from York to Neville Hill carriage sidings, No 55.004** *Queen's Own Highlander* **sets off on its return journey, 'light engine' to Holbeck depot on 13 March 1980. Notice the blanked-off route indicator panel.** *Gavin Morrison*

*Above:*
**No 55.005** *The Prince of Wales Own Regiment of Yorkshire* **rushes out of Welwyn South tunnel on 28 October 1969 in charge of the 12.00 King's Cross–Edinburgh. Notice how the telegraph wires follow the lie of the land over the tunnel. The train is formed of one of the early batches of Mk II coaches.** *J. H. Cooper-Smith*

*Below:*
**Panning alongside Finsbury Park Depot is No 55.006** *The Fife & Forfar Yeomanry* **getting into its stride underneath the wires at the head of the 16.00 King's Cross–Edinburgh on 30 July 1977. This train was the 'Talisman' and the building to the right was actually the old Western Sidings carriage shed, which at that time maintained the Finsbury Park allocation of diesel multiple units.** *Gavin Morrison*

*Above right:*
***Pinza*, No 55 007 looks in fine external condition as she heads the 09.00 Aberdeen–King's Cross past Clifton just north of York on 9 May 1978. Notice the Mk 1 catering vehicle in the centre of the rake of Mk 2D coaches.** *Gavin Morrison*

*Below right:*
**The throttle of No. 55.008** *The Green Howards* **will be wide open passing milepost 185 at Bishopthorpe, three miles south of York as she gathers speed with the 15.50 semi-fast York–King's Cross on 27 June 1981. The grilles for the four radiator fans, two per engine, can be clearly seen.** *Gavin Morrison*

*Left:*
***Crepello,** No 55.012 takes a rest on Sunday 31 July 1977 in the yard at King's Cross 'Passenger Loco' before heading north later in the day. Behind the locomotive are seen the fuel storage tanks.*
*Gavin Morrison*

*Below left:*
**Paying a visit to its original 'home' depot No 55.013 *The Black Watch* poses in the yard at Haymarket in its last year of service on 21 April 1981. By this time she was allocated to York.** *Gavin Morrison*

*Below:*
**Class 03 diesel-mechanical shunter No 03.089 is stabled at the far side of Bradford Exchange ready for shunting duties in the late evening, as No 55.014 *The Duke of Wellington's Regiment* is about to depart with the 17.30 departure to King's Cross on 26 March 1979.**
*Gavin Morrison*

*Above:*
**The up 'Flying Scotsman' nears the end of its journey as it emerges from Gas Works tunnel and enters King's Cross terminus headed by No 55.015 *Tulyar* on 10 July 1976.**
*Gavin Morrison*

*Right:*
**The 'Deltic' that received the most thorough Heavy General Repair in 1975 is seen here after the work was completed. No 55.016 *Gordon Highlander* leaving Peascliffe Tunnel at a speed well over 90mph with the 09.00 King's Cross–Edinburgh on 27 May 1978**
*Gavin Morrison*

*Above:*
**No 55.017 *The Durham Light
Infantry*** **heads a line of
withdrawn locomotives at York,
and the others consist of
Nos 46.027, 40.111 and 40.070. It
was thought that this was
probably the end for the 'Deltic'
too, but she did survive another
visit to Doncaster Works and
was in fact the last 'Deltic' to
receive attention at the 'Plant'
whilst still in BR service. The
date is 1 June 1981.**
*Gavin Morrison*

*Left:*
**A fine study of No 55.018
*Ballymoss*** **and her
surroundings, as she crosses
over from slow to main lines at
Bridge Junction, heading the
13.30 Leeds—King's Cross, after
stopping at Doncaster on 4 April
1977** *Gavin Morrison*

*Left:*
**The 14.50 King's Cross—Leeds races north under the wires through the northern London suburbs at Hadley Wood with** *Royal Highland Fuslier*, **No 55.019 in charge on 19 September 1980.**
*Gavin Morrison*

*Below left:*
**Having worked from King's Cross to Harrogate in the morning, No 55.020** *Nimbus* **is seen in March Lane cutting Leeds approaching Neville Hill carriage sidings with the empty stock on 4 June 1977.**
*Gavin Morrison*

*Below:*
**The up 'Newcastle Executive' passes non stop through Doncaster on its journey from King's Cross and is seen approaching Bridge Junction, with Doncaster Works ('The Plant') along with Doncaster Power Station in the background. No 55.021,** *Argyll & Sutherland Highlander* **was in charge on 2 June 1977. Notice that the train contains two catering vehicles, a practice often adopted to allow the crews to change over their equipment and supplies prior to one vehicle being sent for a main works overhaul; this saved having two vehicles out of traffic for this work to be undertaken, often the only alternative.** *Gavin Morrison*

*Above:*

**Undoubtably Haymarket's favourite 'Deltic' was No 55.022, the erstwhile D9000** *Royal Scots Grey* **as this locomotive often found its way onto trains on special occasions, and leaving from the Scottish end of the ECML. Here she is seen at the head of the up 'Flying Scotsman' about to leave Newcastle Central on 1 May 1978. Notice the restoration of the 'Thistle' headboard, this being the 50th anniversary of the first non stop run of this most famous of famous named trains.** *I. S. Carr*

*Right:*

**As explained in this chapter the operation of the night sleeping car trains was as much a part of the 'Deltic' operation as the day time workings. On an extremely wet night No 55.017** *The Durham Light Infantry* **is ready to depart from King's Cross with the 22.15 'Night Aberdonian' on 10 June 1980. The sleeping coaches are at the rear of the train.** *Gavin Morrison*

*Above:*
**A leak on the steam heating pipe is clearly seen in this photograph of No 55.021 *Argyll & Sutherland Highlander* as she is about to set forth into the night from King's Cross on 10 June 1980.** *Gavin Morrison*

*Left:*
**No 55.015 *Tulyar* awaits departure time with the 20.25 Edinburgh Waverley–King's Cross night train on 6 September 1981. Notice the commemorative plaque between the indicator lights indicating the locomotive's participation in the 'Rocket 150' celebrations at Rainhill the previous year.** *A. Taylor*

# 5
# Keeping Up With The Times

During the 1970s the 'Deltics' must have vindicated their purchase over and over again. The trains they hauled had been progressively accelerated as track improvements were completed. With the High Speed and Advanced Passenger trains (HST and APT) then on the horizon there was no prospect of more 'Deltics' or any further development of them or any other locomotive. It was the ECML's intensive service that halted the further accelerations because many trains had to have Class 47 haulage sometimes because a 'Deltic' was not available, and their lower power and top speed left no room for further margins or even good timekeeping.

Nevertheless the Great Northern suburban electrification with resulting improvements on the last few miles from Hitchin to King's Cross, nor forgetting the formerly severely restricted throat area outside the terminus, together with more 100mph maximum line speeds in Scotland did allow one or two marginal improvements towards the end of the fleet's exclusive and intensive use on the top link services.

In the early 1970s the question of heavy general repairs or refurbishment was on the agenda for all the BR diesel types with an estimated long-term future. Naturally thoughts turned to the 'Deltics'. Over the years these locomotives, like all the other classes, had been repaired over and over again; indeed the original classified repair interval of six months was the shortest of any. However, the work undertaken at these repairs, and in common with all the other types, had been very largely confined to the moving mechanical and electrical parts, engines generators motors auxiliary machines and the like. Little attention had been given to the bodies except for minor repairs and the occasional locomotive damaged in a collision or other accident. Electrical wiring for instance had been given little attention, along with other non-moving parts like fuel and water tanks, doors windows and roof sections to name but a few. After 10 or more years of intensive service and the considerable vibration present from the Deltic engines, a certain amount of body deterioration and fracturing was accumulating. Steps would need to be taken to both eradicate this and prevent its reoccurance, if the fleet were to remain in traffic much longer. By the middle of the 1970s it had become increasingly difficult to maintain the cabs waterproof, and draughts were a major source of complaint from enginemen during the winter months. The sliding doors and windows which were a unique feature of the 'Deltics' were a nightmare to maintain and spares almost impossible to obtain. The windows were not unknown to fall out complete with their frames, when the locomotive was en route! Like a lot of other components the detail parts had become obsolete and had to be specially made, either at great expense and enormously long delivery times, or in railway workshops. Doncaster made brave efforts in this sphere as staff grappled with unfamiliar

tasks, sometimes with extremely successful results, other times not quite so successful. Quite often the original component manufacturers just did not want to know, no longer had the drawings, or had gone out of business and completely passed from the scene. Alternatives were very often tried, usually with some success but rarely as effective as the originals. This is a common problem, not just with the 'Deltics' but now prevalent on other members of BR's ageing diesel classes. Of course, nothing annoys crews more than having to work in damp and draughty conditions.

It was anticipated in 1971 that the class would have a life until around 1986, and this being the case major body attention would be necessary in the period 1975–8. Despite these predictions not a lot of work was carried out to determine the extent of the repairs needed and, when No 55.016 was in Doncaster works for a normal classified repair in 1975, and the body was found to be in such rough condition, a decision was taken to commence the heavy general repair (HGR) programme there and then. Work started in the autumn very much on a 'lets see what we find basis' which was, of course, quite logical, there being little point repairing parts that did not need attention. As events turned out this locomotive was the only one to have the full HGR repair in view of the later decision to shorten the life scale of the fleet and the high costs involved.

However, before these decisions were taken, and in order to ascertain the extent of the repairs needed, it was decided to strip down the body of No 55.016 completely and carry out a total electrical re-wire. The latter being an enormous job by any standards and not repeated on any other members of the class, not least in view of the relatively good condition the existing wiring was found to be in. From the 'prototype' HGR a policy could, it was hoped, be formulated for the remainder of the class.

Generally the inner body skin was found to be in good condition and sound, but there was much corrosion on the outer skin and, as was to be expected, around the doors and windows. There was much rusting and deterioration in the nose-end compartments and many fractures had occurred in the vicinity of the front cab windows. The roof sections too were badly rusted. Concurrently with this work, many of the by now redundant parts were removed, items like sand gear – long out of use – water scoop operating gear, route indicators and the like. The opportunity was also taken to redesign the cab sliding windows, both to overcome the supply problem already highlighted and to fit a more sturdy and less troublesome component. The ever problematical sliding doors had their running tracks completely renewed and, generally speaking it was thereafter no longer necessary for crews to carry a fish-plate around in the cabs. A standard track

fish-plate was just the right size to fit between closed door and pillar to prevent it opening of its own accord due to a warped or rotten body side! Much other work was undertaken on No 55.016 at ths time, far too numerous to itemize.

Experience with this HGR resulted in a list of work considered necessary for the remainder of the fleet to keep them serviceable in to the 1980s. At the same time it was agreed that the condition of the inner body skin was such that no other locomotive should have any attention to it and, likewise no other locomotive got a complete re-wire. It is perhaps opportune here to mention, that it was because of the amount of work undertaken on this locomotive that it later became such a strong contender for preservation.

Only five members of the fleet got a HGR repair, No 55.019 following 55.016 and getting almost as much work done on it except the inner skin and re-wire, and the remainder, Nos 55.002, 55.013 and 55.021 geting successively pruned down versions as the life-span of the class came more and more in question. All these four locomotives had work commenced on them in 1976, and after them it was decided to revert to the standard of the former intermediate repair, albeit with a number of the more important modifications incorporated.

For example, it was argued successfully that the cabside window and sliding door improvements should go ahead along with the removal of the route indicators and the body outer skin repairs where needed. A further important modification which I am detailing because it illustrates how what appears to be a minor item can cause a major failure, concerned the original twin window wipers. Wear and tear on the linkage that coupled the two blades had a bad habit of tieing itself in knots, usually when it was pouring with rain and, if on the driver's side, causing a major in-traffic casualty. Again the manufacturers of these mechanisms had ceased to make them, and unless BR ordered hundreds were not prepared to go into production again, so single blades were substituted. They were not as effective, but experience proved them to be adequate and drivers eventually accepted them.

It was in the later 1970s that the overhauled and repaired engine supply situation became the most acute. Locomotives often languished in Doncaster Works minus the most essential components for months and even years. It was a spare part supply problem mainly connected with pistons which had usually resulted in a fractured crankcase. Indeed in 1978 the Mk 1V bolted crown pistons were having to be examined at 3,000hr – which necessitated complete engine strip down – because of the little end problems already mentioned. To help the supply situation some of the old design Mk 111 pistons were pressed into service but these had to be examined – again-meaning a complete engine strip down – at but 2,000hr. These premature overhauls were preferred to the risk of a 'leg out of bed' and resultant scrap crankcase. It was during this period that the specialist technical riding inspectors came into their own by keeping a close watch on suspect engines, very often riding on the same locomotive day after day and noting their 'breathing' under load. Many were the occasions when engines were withdrawn from service or shut down en route and expensive failures prevented. Equally a precious additional few hours could sometimes be got out of an engine, keeping a locomotive in traffic until Doncaster had a repaired engine ready to fit. I cannot over-emphasise how important all these measures were to keep the fleet running at such an availability in their later years of intensive use; but it was at a high cost in time and effort.

Such was the magnitude of the engine problem that from

January 1979 the fleet diagrammed availability was reduced to 50% from an already low 64%; yes a mere 11 of the 22 locomotives in traffic each day. Even with these measures actual availability in early 1979 was but 42%; Class 47s were meanwhile struggling to keep the schedules. By 1980 there was some improvement and diagrammed availability increased to 55%.

Another job undertaken on the fleet during the period under review was a campaign replacement of both coolant and oil cooling radiators. The originals and their float of spares had been cleaned over and over again both internally and externally; they were well past their best. The cooling of the engine coolant in a 'Deltic' had always been critical as the radiator capacity and air flow was only just sufficient to prevent boiling during periods of high ambient temperatures. Depots had to pay particular attention to keeping radiators clean inside and out, as well as paying strict attention to the cooling fans, their drives and clutches. During hot summers there would always be some casualties due to high water temperature despite the attention given. One of the inherent problems with the class, and many of the English Electric built locomotives suffered, was the arrangement for driving the radiator fans. There were four in the case of the 'Deltic' locomotive, two for each engine. It is a great arrangement for simplicity, but when an engine is returned to its idling speed, perhaps when the locomotive has just breasted a long climb, the fan speed also drops at a time when the latent heat from the engine is most in need of dissipation. This result is an immediate and steep rise in the coolant temperature and the fans are unable to draw sufficient air through the radiators to cope because of their low speed, so the system boils and before long the engine will shut down with a low coolant level, and a casualty occurs.

In 1975 a system of internal flow testing and external air testing was devised at Doncaster to detect the build up of internal scale and external deterioration which no amount of washing with all sorts of acids seemed able to dislodge. The radiators were progressively replaced as soon as possible after testing and as replacements became available, the known bad ones first. At the same time it was also decided to replace the smaller oil radiators because, albeit to a lesser extent, they had started to give problems too. Much of the actual replacement of the radiators was carried out at the owning depots as it was a job well within their capability. Fortunately this replacement programme was well under way before the very hot summer of 1976 and the problems, in the main, disappeared, provided the radiators were kept clean.

To keep the record straight, mention must be made of the loss of the locomtives rather pleasing (in your author's view) two-tone green livery. The all-over 'rail-blue' was substituted in the late 1960s as the locomotives received classified repairs. The new five figure TOPS numbers were applied by the depots commencing with No 9020 (The 'D' prefix had already been removed after the final demise of steam traction on British Rail in 1968) which was renumbered No 55.020 in November 1973, and completed with No 9010 which became 55.010 in June the following year. No 9000 was renumbered 55.022 because in the new scheme there were no numbers allocated ending with a zero, otherwise they were renumbered consecutively with the 55 prefix denoting their class.

One pleasant aspect of these later years of their intensive utilisation was the re-introduction of a train carrying the name 'Silver Jubilee', in this case to celebrate the 25th anniversary of the reign of Her Majesty Queen Elizabeth 2. The original

'Silver Jubilee' train had made history on 27 September, 1935, when during a trial run prior to introduction into ordinary service, the fully streamlined seven coach train achieved a speed of 112½mph, then a record for this country. It was hauled by a brand new Gresley 'A4' Pacific No 2509 *Silver Link*. The train went into service between King's Cross and Newcastle on 30 September, 1935, and was named in celebration of the Silver Jubilee of Their Majesties King George V and Queen Mary. It left Newcastle at 10.00 each weekday being due in London at 14.00, returning from the capital at 17.30 the train was due in the Tyneside city at 21.30. This gave an average speed in both directions of 70.4mph which was some achievement in those days and the precursor of a new era in rail travel. As the first of the streamlined trains in this country it built up an excellent punctuality record and became a legend in its own short life. It ceased to run, never to return, with the outbreak of the war in Europe in late 1939.

It was a nice idea, therefore, to re-introduce this train name and on this occasion the trains chosen were the 07.45 King's Cross–Edinburgh and the 15.00 return service. Special locomotive headboards were made together with coach destination indicators and restaurant car menus, napkins and much other paraphernalia. Indeed a special train set was kept for the diagram and the restaurant car was tastefully fitted out with memorabillia of ECML times past. The train started to carry its new name on Wednesday 8 June 1977 after the May Bank Holiday and continued to do so for the remainder of that year. No 55.012 did the honours on the inaugural down journey and despite the fact that the diagrams showed the same locomotive as working the train in both directions, Haymarket were not going to let Finsbury Park steal all the thunder, and their No 55.022 was at the head of the up train. Both trains had champagne send-offs from their respective termini.

I recall with some amusement the efforts we often had to go to so as to ensure the headboards were always carried by the locomotives. I think I am correct in remembering that a total of 12 were made, half to suit the 'Deltics' and just in case, the other half to suit Class 47s. Of course, being the first departure from London each morning it was extremely unlikely a 'Deltic' would not be available, shortages usually occurred later in the day. However, there was always the possibility of a substitution en route or at Edinburgh, and this sometimes happened, some of the headboards were located at Gateshead in case of engine changes at Newcastle. What often happened was the boards beginning to collect all in the one place, as people forgot to return them if locomotives got out of diagram or whatever. Rapid phone calls, sometimes over a weekend as the train ran Monday–Friday only, resulted in consignments of headboards being loaded into brake vans or the back cabs of locomotives as order was restored ready for the next days departures! I think some 'official' was very often posted on the platform at York as the trains were due to ensure the headboard was carried, it was usually a little after the train was due to pass there that the phone would ring if no headboard was on the front of the locomotive!

The operation of this train turned out to be the last highlight in the 'Deltics' career as the premier East Coast motive power, and they operated it with distinction. The very next year it became the first regular train on this line, by then unnamed of course, to be formed of a HST set as a prelude to their full introduction.

*Below:*
**Five members of the class, Nos 55.002,13,16,19 and 21 received Heavy General Repairs (HGRs) during 1975 and 1976. In this picture No 55.0002** *The King's Own Yorkshire Light Infantry* **is seen in Doncaster Works receiving its repair, whilst on the right is No 55.016** *Gordon Highlander.* **This locomotive was in the 'Plant' for some more minor attention having received its HGR some time previous to this photograph taken on 3 October 1976**
*Gavin Morrison*

## The Heavy General Repair Locomotives

*Above:*
**No 55.013 *The Black Watch*
rushes towards King's Cross as
she passes Hadley Wood on
19 September 1980 at the head
of the 12.35 ex Hull. The cleaner
lines after removal of the sand
boxes will be noticed.**
*Gavin Morrison*

*Left:*
**No 55.016 *Gordon Highlander*
rounds the bend in the cutting
at Sunderland Bridge with an up
express on 30 May 1978.**
*Gavin Morrison*

*Right:*
The down 'Talisman' emerges from under the magnificent roof at York as it leaves Platform 9 headed by No 55.019 *Royal Highland Fusilier* on 15 August 1977. *Gavin Morrison*

## King's Cross—Doncaster

*Below:*
The external condition of No 55.021 *Argyll & Sutherland Highlander* hardly does credit to Haymarket depot as she leans on the curve at Clifton, north of York, heading the 14.00 King's Cross—Edinburgh on 5 April 1978. The oil on the side of the body is carry-over from the engine via its exhaust.
*Gavin Morrison*

*Left:*
**No 55.018 *Ballymoss* starts up the second engine as she prepares to leave King's Cross with the 16.05 semi-fast to York on 20 May 1981. The white cab proclaims this as one of the Finsbury Park allocation**
*Gavin Morrison*

*Below:*
**The Sundays only 09.45 King's Cross—Edinburgh climbs Holloway Bank at the start of its journey headed by No 55.010 *The King's Own Scottish Borderer* on 31 July 1977**
*Gavin Morrison*

*Above:*
**No 55.002 *The King's Own Yorkshire Light Infantry* rushes towards Peascliffe Tunnel at the head of the morning Cleethorpes–King's Cross train on 12 September 1980** *Gavin Morrison*

*Above right:*
**The new alignment of the ECML south of Doncaster had not quite been completed when No 55.010 *The King's Own Scottish Borderer***

**approached Bridge Junction with the 12.05 King's Cross–York semi-fast on 26 March 1981.**
*Gavin Morrison*

*Right:*
**The up 'Newcastle Executive' passes non stop through Doncaster on 8 June 1977 with No 55.014 *The Duke of Wellington's Regiment* at its head**
*Gavin Morrison*

## Doncaster-Leeds- Bradford-Harrogate

*Above:*
Having left the ECML just north of Doncaster station the 11.25 from King's Cross heads towards Leeds near Carcroft headed by No 55.021 *Argyll & Sutherland Highlander* on 4 April 1977. *Gavin Morrison*

*Below:*
The 17.30 Leeds–King's Cross makes rapid progress through Fitzwilliam with No 55.018 *Ballymoss* on 8 May 1977. Note the small dots in the indicator panel which distinguished this

locomotive from the remainder of the fleet at this period. *Gavin Morrison*

*Right:*
No 55.010 *The King's Own Scottish Borderer* in immaculate condition passes under Tinsley viaduct on the outskirts of Leeds on 8 May 1977 with the 12.30 Leeds–King's Cross. *Gavin Morrison*

*Below right:*
It is hard to believe that in this photograph No 55.016 *Gordon Highlander*, heading the 10.45 Leeds–King's Cross is passing the site of the former Copley Hill steam locomotive shed on 25 July 1980 *Gavin Morrison*

*Above:*
**The 09.10 train from King's Cross approaches Leeds City on 8 February 1977 headed by No 55.010** *The King's Own Scottish Borderer;* **this locomotive would be diagrammed to return to the capital with the 12.30 departure.** *Gavin Morrison*

*Right:*
**No 55.020** *Nimbus* **heads the 11.25 King's Cross–Harrogate past Armley in the outskirts of Leeds on 4 June 1977.**
*Gavin Morrison*

*Below right:*
**Following on from the previous illustration,** *Nimbus* **returns from Harrogate with the empty coaches to Neville Hill carriage sidings for maintenance.**
*Gavin Morrison*

73

## Doncaster-Edinburgh

*Above:*
**The 15.50 York—King's Cross semi-fast takes the platform road off the Selby swing bridge as it prepares to stop on 14 April 1981 headed by No 55.021 *Argyll & Sutherland Highlander*.** *Gavin Morrison*

*Right:*
**Selby South Junction sees the passing of the 14.05 King's Cross—York headed by No 55.022 *Royal Scots Grey* on 14 April 1981** *Gavin Morrison*

*Below right:*
**No 55.020 *Nimbus* is dwarfed by the massive arched roof of York station as she approaches with the 09.30 Newcastle—King's Cross on 14 September 1977.** *Gavin Morrison*

*Above:*
**Seen from under the roof of Darlington Bank top station is the down 'Flying Scotsman' carrying its reporting number 1S17, and headed by No D9020 *Nimbus* as it roars past on the avoiding line in April 1971.**
*M. Dunnett*

*Centre left:*
**Two up trains from King's Cross side by side at Newcastle Central on 8 August 1964. No D9004 *Queen's Own Highlander* heads the 'Flying Scotsman' and is about to leave platform 9 complete with 'thistle' headboard, whilst Brush Type 4 (Later Class 47) No D1506 is waiting to leave platform 8 with a Newcastle–King's Cross train. All the original 20 Class 47s were allocated to ECML workings when new, from Finsbury Park.** *J. S. Hancock*

*Left:*
**The 11.52 King's Cross–Edinburgh train negotiates the extremely sharp curve through Morpeth station with No 9006 *The Fife & Forfar Yeomanry* on 17 July 1970. This location has, unfortunately been in the news on more than one occasion due to serious derailments as a result of excessive speed.**
*I. S. Carr*

*Above:*
**Having crossed the Royal Border Bridge into Scotland, No 55.004** *Queen's Own Highlander* **passes along what is probably the most scenic section of the ECML, just north of Lamberton Beach with the 12.00 King's Cross—Aberdeen on 6 August 1977.**
*Gavin Morrison*

*Right:*
**After the disastrous collapse of the Penmanshiel Tunnel in 1979 the through express trains on the ECML which continued to run through to Edinburgh, were diverted via Carlisle to join the WCML and then ran via Carstairs. However, some trains terminated short of their journeys and a shuttle service was operated between Newcastle and Berwick, and between Edinburgh and Dunbar. The 'Deltics' were regularly used on both the through services and the shuttles, and here No 55.009** *Alycidon* **is seen leaving Edinburgh Waverley with the 17.15 shuttle to Dunbar on 4 August 1979. Later in the day, this locomotive would head one of the night sleeping car trains south, as all these workings continued to run through between the two cities via Carlisle. The departure time is shown clearly on the clock surmounting the North British Hotel.** *Gavin Morrison*

## The 'Silver Jubilee'

*Above:*
The down 'Silver Jubilee' approaches Dringhouses Yard on the outskirts of York headed by No 55.013 *The Black Watch* on 19 September 1977. *Gavin Morrison*

*Left:*
No 55.007 *Pinza* accelerates round the curve at Clifton just north of York on 23 September 1977 with the down 'Silver Jubilee'. *Gavin Morrison*

*Below:*
This picture clearly shows the attractive headboard, one of several specially made for this service. The down train is seen here leaving York on 14 September 1977 headed by No 55.019 *Royal Highland Fusilier*. Notice that the locomotive carries its running number at both ends, and at this time this was the only 'Deltic' with this feature. *Gavin Morrison*

# 6
# Living With The 'Deltics'

One day glancing through the Inter-Regional vacancy list I noticed the Traction Maintenance & Plant Engineer's job at Finsbury Park advertised. At that time I was working at Crewe and I had always been on the London Midland Region. I knew little or nothing about Finsbury Park, except that it was a main line diesel locomotive depot on the Eastern Region's Great Northern main line into London. I felt I needed a change and the 'Big City' seemed as good a place as any, so I applied.

After being summoned for an interview I recall trying to find out as much as I could about the 'Deltics'. I also remember being told at the interview that they would not ask me about this class because I would have no knowledge! So it was that I found myself appointed to the post and I journeyed south to take up the appointment in the late summer of 1974.

The original Eastern Region, before combining with the North Eastern, had organised itself well for the new main line diesel locomotives introduced under the modernisation plan. New purpose built depots were constructed, all of a similar design, and they were clean, airy, light and well built structures incorporating much thought. Eventually such depots appeared at Stratford, March, Immingham, Tinsley and the doyen of them all, Finsbury Park. This was the first one actually commissioned. Unfortunately there was comparatively little experience to draw on regarding maintenance of the new traction when these new depots were being planned and built. Consequently, drawbacks were discovered later and there were a few 'white elephants'. However, there is absolutely no doubt it was the right way to go and the Eastern Region benefitted where some other Regions suffered and many of the depots are still giving excellent service today.

One of the complexities at the King's Cross end of the Great Northern was the intense use of the tracks leading out of the station and through Gas Works tunnel towards Holloway and beyond. This had been a problem from early times and when extensions to the suburban platforms necessitated removal of the small locomotive facility, there were even more light engine movements between the station and the goods yard, north of Gas Works tunnel where the famous Top Shed was situated. To alleviate some of these movements additional land had to be purchased, a canal diverted and much excavation done, and this resulted in a extremely cramped locomotive yard and servicing facility to the north-west of the station platforms. This enabled many of the 'foreign' engines working into and out of the terminus to be serviced and turned without congesting the tracks to and from Top Shed. The problem was still evident in diesel times and as well as a new depot at Finsbury Park it was felt necessary to adapt 'King's Cross Passenger Loco', as it was universally called (or sometimes just 'The Passenger Loco'), to service the new forms of traction too. Fuel tanks were installed and a small

shed built where the smaller 'Daily' (late 'A') examinations could be carried out and minor repairs undertaken at servicing periods. For a short period this depot served both types of traction but as steam was phased out the turntable was removed and the siding accommodation increased so that locomotives could await their next turns. Hornsey Depot was also retained to service those locomotives utilised on local empty coach workings to and from the various sidings, and thus keep them away from the congested 'Passenger Loco' and Finsbury Park unless absolutely necessary. Occasionally 'train locomotives' would be utilised on an ECS working between trains, but this was extremely rare for a 'Deltic' so they would not visit Hornsey during the normal course of affairs.

One of the major difficulties with the 'Passenger Loco' was the tight curvature of the tracks leading in and out. This often resulted in derailments, and as a derailed locomotive usually resulted in not only trapping others, but also in effectively stopping the whole depot from working correctly, pandemonium would reign and locomotives would have to be ferried to either Hornsey or Finsbury Park for servicing. However, the Finsbury Park breakdown gang would soon be in attendance and latterly by using road transport they would not be long; additonally a small amount of re-railing equipment was kept at the depot and the local staff would commence the re-railing operations pending arrival of the proper gang; over a period they became quite competent. It is perhaps worth mentioning that because of the sharp curves the 1Co-Co1 locomotives (Classes 40, 45 and 46), were never *officially* allowed to visit the 'Passenger Loco', and should always have gone to either Hornsey or Finsbury Park for servicing – operating dictates, however, often found them being serviced at King's Cross.

One of the reasons behind these various arrangements was to leave Finsbury Park to concentrate on the larger examinations and repairs without the added problems of a large throughput of locomotives for servicing and minor attention. Its eventual allocation of main line locomotives being well in excess of 100. At the time of my arrival the 'Passenger Loco' was servicing something in the region of 40 locomotives per shift, making anything up to 120–130 locomotives per 24hr period. By this time Hornsey Depot had closed and the locomotives engaged on ECS working were being serviced at Finsbury Park, around 50 a day. To accommodate this additional workload a separate exit road had been incorporated in the depot layout as well as extra stabling sidings. At this time a number of the suburban services were still locomotive-hauled, indeed the Great Northern was the last suburban route to use non-corridor locomotive hauled coaches, and these locomotives too, were being serviced at Finsbury Park.

By 1974 among the problems arising from the operating

requirements of the ECML was the difference in train formations between day and night services. From the 07.45 King's Cross–Newcastle – then the first daytime northbound departure – to the last down Newcastle at 19.40, every main line passenger train leaving London was air-braked and electrically heated. Conversely, the other side of these hours all trains were vacuum-braked and steam-heated. The necessity for intensive utilisation since dieselisation had resulted in the locomotives used on the day trains also being used on the night ones; for example the locomotive that brought the 10.00 ex Edinburgh (the 'Flying Scotsman') into King's Cross, could return north after servicing with one of the night sleeping car trains. This would have been easy if all the trains had been compatible, but as they were not, it made it necessary to have a fleet of locomotives both dual-heated and dual-braked with the result that the 'Deltics' had to retain their temperamental Spanner Mk 11 boilers.

Generally speaking the Spanner boiler is the simplest and most reliable, but the Mk 11 was without doubt the black sheep of the family. It was a struggle to keep them going latterly when the only possibility of actually riding with them in the service conditions so necessary to eliminate faults was at night. Finsbury Park bred a breed of nocturnal technical assistants to perform that function; a very basic training for some BR engineering managers of today, who cut their teeth on this thankless task!

Unlike the West Coast route, the ECML continued into diesel days with both the Eastern and Scottish Regions sharing the motive power requirements for the Anglo-Scottish trains. To this end Haymarket Depot in Edinburgh had its share of the 'Deltic' fleet, and later some dual-heated and dual-braked Class 47s too. But the London end of the line always had to find a larger proportion of locomotives each morning with its commitments for both English provincial city trains as well as the Anglo-Scottish ones; there were early morning departures to places like Newcastle, Leeds, Bradford, Cleethorpes and Hull. If the correct types of locomotives had not powered the overnight trains, then by lunch time there was trouble. Only to often steam-heat Class 40s and 47s came southwards overnight, resulting in a struggle by mid-day to provide suitable power before the first of the early morning Up trains had had their locomotives released and serviced for the return journey. Occasionally dual-heated Class 31s – intended for ECS workings normally – had to be hurriedly sent north to deputise; but with only 1,470bhp to play with there would be a considerable loss of time-keeping. However, sometimes it was possible to spare two such machines in which case a spirited performance would result. Generally speaking though, power controllers were reluctant to do this as, very often only one locomotive would return! Meanwhile, the unwanted Class 40 or whatever, would while away its time until being sent 'home' that night.

Provision of power at King's Cross was always extremely tight even without incidents like those outlined above, but a fine group of staff existed at the 'Passenger Loco', outbased from Finsbury Park itself, and they were well trained in keeping as many locomotives in traffic, without them having to go to Finsbury Park. Unfortunately, it was not possible to renew brake blocks at King's Cross in view of the time taken and the pit space it would occupy. Thus, the majority of 'knock outs' were for brake block renewal. When I arrived around four sets of locomotive brake blocks were being renewed per shift, excluding those renewed during the scheduled larger examinations on the Finsbury Park fleet itself. With 24 brake

blocks consisting a set this amounted to over 1,000 brake blocks a week and kept at least six men employed seven days a week for the full 24 hours each day; this made the depot one of the largest users of brake blocks on the Eastern Region, and one of the largest on BR as a whole. Incidentally, the combined King's Cross and Finsbury Park Depots were also the largest user of diesel fuel on the Region.

To assist in turn-rounds at King's Cross when power was tight, use would be made of the 'Pilot' locomotive kept there – usually a Class 31 – and this could be used to shunt-release locomotives from incoming trains that were normally allowed to remain at the buffer stops until the coaches they had brought in departed north again. This would give quicker locomotive turn-rounds and it assisted the Running Foreman's practice of 'stepping-up'. This is when locomotives are successively utilised on earlier departures than diagrammed, and all generally goes well provided everybody realises there is an end, and makes provision for a locomotive for the last train! If the overnight trains were late arriving in London for whatever reason, their locomotives were very often shunt-released so that they could be serviced to take up their diagrammed north-bound workings.

It would be on occasions when no final answer could be seen to the power problems that Regional Control at York would be asked to come to the rescue. However, having a depot with its own allocation at the end of the line would often pay dividends because locomotives would be released off examinations and repairs at all times of the day and night, and could make all the differance. Thus, allowing for a proportion of the Region's 'stopped' locomotive target to be at terminal points was a critical part of the overall strategy. If too many locomotives were 'stopped' at one depot, another depot could help out by adjusting its examination programme. Sometimes locomotives in need of repairs to particular components could be kept in traffic on 'restricted working'. For example, if there were problems with the steam train heating apparatus, the locomotive could be confined to ETH working or even freight trains; likewise a vacuum brake fault could see a locomotive restricted to working air-braked trains only. All these factors could help to provide locomotives over periods of power shortage, sometimes just a few hours, on rarer occasions for several days.

It will be imagined from the foregoing that any estimated release times quoted during the morning 'call-over', that would give availability to the operator that same day, had to be as accurate as possible because, very often, power controllers would plan to use the released locomotive shortly after its estimated release time. Regional Control would of course oversee the whole situation, and if all else failed, additional power – sometimes two or even three locomotives coupled together – would be worked up to King's Cross from wherever it was available. Very often, if a 'Deltic' was released from Doncaster Works during the day and provided another was not running around in need of works attention, in which case a changeover would sometimes be arranged in Doncaster station, it would be worked light to King's Cross to take up a diagram.

I have dealt at length with the problems encountered in the King's Cross area because they were so much a part of the 'Deltic' story. I feel they are essential to form a background picture of both the railway they operated, and the maintenance facilities that partly existed to maintain them. When I arrived on the scene I think the first thing that impressed me was the high esteem in which the fleet was held,

not just by those directly involved with them, but by almost everybody. Nobody referred to them by their proper numbers, by which the more mundane diesel types were known, simply 'No 7' or 'No 10'; speak of 'No 22' and nobody was in any doubt as to what you were referring to. At Finsbury Park we had the racehorses, and what excellent names for a fleet of locomotives engaged on top-link express work, and a continuation of a fine East Coast tradition too.

I soon discovered that the sort of working day I was going to have was directly proportional to the number of locomotives queueing at the fuel point in a morning. These could be seen, and more significantly counted, as I walked along Isledon Road on my way to the depot. Two or three and it was nothing to worry about, many more usually meant problems because these would be the locomotives that had powered the overnight trains and had had to be 'knocked out' at King's Cross for attention. Power would be tight all day and the pressure would be on to repair and release as many locomotives as possible.

The system by which the 'Deltic' fleet was maintained was new to me, keeping such a small fleet at a high rate of availability and reliability needed some organisation and the pressure was on all the time. For example, a locomotive that had worked one of the up overnight trains and arrived in London at around 05.30, would very often be shunt-released and sent to Finsbury Park for examination. The 06.00 shift staff would be undertaking pre-examination brake and running tests by the time I arrived on duty at 08.00. Additional staff would be deployed from the 08.00 shift once any problems or repairs had been identified. If it was one of the smaller 'B' examinations, it could be expected that the afternoon shift would complete the work required and the locomotive would return north again that evening or night. In early days this sort of arrangement had actually been included in one of the diagrams and the locomotive in question was booked to work the down afternoon 'Talisman' – 16.00 ex King's Cross – it was some achievement.

The depots had an excellent back-up in the Doncaster Works stores organisation. The procedure known as Urgent Vehicle Standing (UVS) is used when material is urgently needed for a locomotive. Despite the stocks held at the depots there are always items that are in short supply for all number of reasons; for instance there might have recently been a heavy demand for a particular component, the manufacturer might not have delivered in accordance with his promises or whatever. Of course there were also items that depots did not normally stock due to a low requirement, but which very occasionally were needed. Whatever the circumstances, if word reached Doncaster before lunch it was a pretty safe bet – heavy and bulky items excepted – that the item would be on a train that same afternoon. If it were for us, then the van would be deputed to meet the train and the material would soon find its way onto which ever 'Deltic' needed it. The *esprit de corps* when one mentioned a 'Deltic' was magnificent – everybody knew how vital they were for the train service – but it was all quite new to me.

Maintenance work on the 'Deltics', as I have already made brief mention of, was very often difficult and they were very cramped inside the engine rooms. Indeed any work on the engines themselves, and there was little the depots could do compared with more conventional types of diesel locomotive, was both awkward and in cramped situations. The fitters needed to be real contortionists and spend much of their time either lying on their backs or sides. Battery renewal was one of

the electricians most difficult jobs because the battery was located in the engine room flanking each side of the train heating boiler. It was an awkward job to man-handle the battery blocks, weighing about one cwt each, past the engine and generator unit, then the control cubicle, through the narrow and double engine room doors and then the cab door to get them outside. We were lucky at Finsbury Park because all our shed roads had solebar height platforms; not so Gateshead for instance, and we usually carried out their battery changes for them. With its position in the engine room, suffering extremes of temperature, vibration and a gaseous atmosphere, battery life was generally less than other types of locomotive. However, because of the locomotives intensive use, a flat battery was a rare problem.

In the mid 1970s the general problems associated with thermal cracking of locomotive tyres were at their height after a series of potentially nasty incidents. It had been proved beyond doubt that a thermal hair-line crack on the edge of the tyre could be the precursor of a complete tyre failure, and was often caused by the temperature differentials created by flanging brake blocks. This is a brake block which, because of wear and tear in the brake gear, forces its way over the edge of the tyre tread. As that part of the block still in contact with the tyre wears away, the remainder edges down the side. As well as cracking, with the amount of block being in contact with the tyre tread reduced, so is the brake force available.

The Class 47 presented the biggest problem, not least in view of the large amount of linkage in their brake gear, and a special brake block with a narrower contact area had been specially designed for them in an effort to contain the problem. Other locomotives also suffered and the 'Deltic' was included among them. However, in view of the high speed work undertaken by the 'Deltics' permission was not forthcoming for the use of the 'narrow block' (as it was universally called) developed for the Class 47. Thus, brake blocks were having to be renewed as soon as flanging became apparant and this became more and more frequent as the locomotives got nearer and nearer to classified repairs. This caused much additional depot work renewing brake blocks and also reduced locomotive availability, not to mention constituting a waste of otherwise good brake blocks which had to be renewed well before their normal scrapping size. Because of the design of the compensated brake gear it was always necessary to renew all the brake blocks irrespective of how many were actually flanging, otherwise it was impossible to adjust the brake gear correctly afterwards.

The same problem that existed with the 'Deltics' had also been apparent with the London Midland Region Class 50s, and a further special block had been designed for them with a integral lug cast on its side. This lug bore against a rubbing plate fitted on the bogie and prevented the block from moving out of line with the tyre tread. It was easy to fit the rubbing plates on all inner positions as they were attached to the bolster; however, a modification to the bogies was necessary to provide special brackets for the rubbing plates in the outer positions. When I went to Finsbury Park it was good to get this modification underway on the 'Deltics' and we modified some of the inner positions on the worst locomotives ourselves to get an immediate, albeit restricted improvement. As the locomotives went through Doncaster Works for classified repairs all positions were modified, and this was one of the major factors that allowed the six month frequency for main works repairs to be extended to nine months. Clearly this had considerable beneficial results, both in terms of direct costs

and locomotive availability.

I have dwelt on the subject of brake blocks at length because then, as now, their life is the criterion for BR's main line locomotive fleet having to visit depots. It is one of the deciding factors in examination periodicities and anything that can increase the life of the block is well worthy of investigation.

As a general rule each of the depots with 'Deltics' allocated would try and have only one 'stopped' at a time. The examination periods would bring each individual locomotive in for a 'B', 'C' or 'D' examination after about eight – 10 days in traffic, and over the years this was gradually increased to between 12 and 14 days. (There was no 'E' examination in the 'Deltic' schedule like other types). Unlike the 'A' examination, which would be carried out wherever a locomotive was when it became due, the larger examinations were almost always done at the locomotives 'home' depot. 'B' examinations were usually completed within 24hr provided no large or involved repairs were necessary, but the larger 'C' and 'D' exams would take longer, anything between two and four days. Again however, if anything big was found to need attention, these periods could be extended, particularly as the locomotives got older, and shopping periods were extended.

It was usual at the depots to try and keep an eye on all major components likely to cause trouble or failures, and if at all possible anticipate their renewal. This allowed a little planning as to when the locomotive should be 'stopped', perhaps more importantly time to get the spare parts needed, and to try not to have two locomotives 'stopped' at the same time. This was frequently a finally balanced game, anticipating how long the particular component would hold out. It was in this connection that the Inspectors based on King's Cross station came into their own. It was a policy for them to meet the arrival of each main line train and this way they could keep a special eye on any locomotive that was under observation for the reasons just described. They, along with the Technical Riding Inspectors, were the depot's eyes and ears.

The staff at King's Cross were found over the years to be an essential part of the overall policy. Long experience taught that it was far better to meet trains when the crew could be closely questioned and this was particularly so if some spurious and difficult to locate fault was being investigated. Far better to speak to a driver first hand, than read some hurriedly written note in a repair book. The driver could describe exactly what symptoms he had experienced if the fault had occurred en route, and he might be able to tell the Inspector just that vital piece of information that would set the maintenance staff on the right track. So often faults that crews experienced could not be reproduced when the locomotives were tested statically, try as we might.

A close watch would be kept on tyre wear and advance notice fed to Maintenance Control as locomotives became in need of reprofiling to restore their treads. This work was usually done on the ground wheel lathe at Doncaster Depot, in the main because of its proximity to where the locomotives worked. However, the similar machine – either of which could turn locomotive tyres without taking the wheels from under the locomotive – at the Regional Repair Shop at Stratford was also used. In any event, and almost invariably, such work on 'Deltics' would be arranged for a weekend to avoid reducing weekday availability.

Equal to those at the 'Passenger Loco' was a fine group of staff at Finsbury Park itself, and the nucleus of both groups came from the former Top Shed. I recall a number with special affection, but I have chosen to illustrate just two of them; and I know that none of their erstwhile colleagues will begrudge them special mention.

Eddie Dolata was a boilersmith of Polish extraction and to our advantage remained in this country after the war, marrying an English girl. Eddie was without doubt the finest welder it has ever been my privilege to meet. His reputation spread and many locomotives were brought specially to Finsbury Park for Eddie to undertake some specialist welding task. The exhaust drum collector tanks on the 'Deltics' were good examples of Eddie's skill and where his expertise was invaluable. These tanks were partly made of stainless steel, a difficult material to weld at the best of times. It was almost impossible to get these tanks off the engines and out of the locomotives with the engines in situ and, as outlined earlier they had a propensity to fracture at the welds where the branch exhausts joined the tank itself, even after modification. By undoing all the connections to the tank and unbolting it from the engine, a difficult enough task in itself, it was possible to rotate the drum until the offending cracked seam was uppermost, then Eddie could get at it. The extensive use of aluminium on the locomotives represented no problems to him either.

Charlie Sugrim was an electrician and the finest electrical fault finder I have ever come across. Charlie had an amazing sense of direction in locating the most elusive faults that might have evaded others for literally days. He used to frustrate supervisors, inspectors and fellow electricians alike when he would return from a spell of leave and find some fault they had all been scratching their heads on for hours on end, in just minutes. He knew the 'Deltics' electrical wiring like the proverbial 'back of his hand' and I never knew him lost for a cure for longer than a few hours at the most. Needless to say, everybody breathed a sigh of relief when Eddie and Charlie returned from a spell of leave!

Another problem, which whilst applying to the other diesel locomotives too, is worthy of mention, is water ingress into the compressed air systems. This is bad enough in normal weather conditions as it can cause all sorts of brake faults, but in freezing conditions it can be extremely serious. Often a frozen compressor governor would cause a complete locomotive failure, sometimes out on the line and, as these governors were situated in the nose end compartments they were extemely vulnerable to cold weather. Indeed, with the onset of the winter we used to cover them with a home made case to try and keep the worst of the cold out. There were a number of ways of trying to keep the water out of the system, none were 100% successful. Methylated Spirits could be introduced into the air on its way into the compressor and finding its way throughout the air system, prevent any water trapped in the system from freezing. The quantity introduced could be adjusted to suit conditions by means of a wick, but it was an expensive solution. There was some resistance to its continued use, but on the Eastern Region we persisted, particulary on the 'Deltics', and many an on-line failure was avoided.

A number of other problems encountered with the 'Deltics' over the years are, perhaps worth a mention at this juncture. For example the load regulators were a constant source of trouble, not always causing failures, but requiring much time and effort by the maintenance staff. There were two regulators per locomotive, one for each power unit and they were situated in the respective power cubicles, being operated by an oil driven vane motor which responded to the engine governors. Two flexible oil pipes connected each governor to its own hydraulic regulator controller, and two more flexible

pipes in turn connected this controller to the vane motor. According to engine load the motor would run the regulator to either increase or decrease generator field strength, depending on the actions in the governor itself of the load control valve. This valve reacted to the load on the engine, this in turn depending on the position of the driver's power controller. The load regulator was circular and consisted of a series of static and moving electrical contacts around its perimeter. The vane motor actuated a roller which was pivoted in the centre and by moving the roller around, so different moving contacts would come into and out of contact with their static opposite numbers. Thus, depending on the direction of travel, clockwise or anti-clockwise, generator field excitation would be switched into and out of circuit. When the generator was at full excitation it would develop its full output and when the engine governor sensed the engine was becoming overloaded, by its inability, via the load regulator, to increase generator field strength any more (and hence its power output), it would initiate a stage of traction motor field diversion; this would reduce the load on the generator, hence the load on the engine, and the load regulator would 'run-back' and reduce the generator field strength.

The setting of the clearances between the moving and fixed contacts was critical, and special tools were available to set both the gaps, and the position of the contacts in relation to the roller. Because the regulator roller spent much of its time fluctuating around those contacts in the maximum field strength range (full power), the contacts in that area tended to wear more than the remainder. They would often become pitted and sometimes would even weld together; other times the roller would stick because of damaged contacts and not return to minimum field, in each of these situations the result would very often be the same, a complete loss of power on the power unit concerned once the driver closed the power controller and then tried to apply power again.

Yet another problem with the regulators was a leaking vane motor oil seal and this would allow oil to escape into the regulator itself, contaminating the contacts at the bottom of the regulator and associated windings; again, a loss of power would sometimes ensue. All in all the regulator needed regular skilled attention, the slightest sign of an oil leak during the 'B' examination and the seals would be renewed; likewise the smallest sign of pitting or other damage to the contacts and they would be renewed along with those each side of the suspect ones. A set of the setting tools and spare contacts were kept at the 'Passenger Loco' and many a locomotive was saved a time-consuming trip out to Finsbury Park for the necessary repairs. Of course today, such complex equipment to control the electrical load of diesel-electric locomotives is completely obsolete, one small 'electronic box' will do all that is necessary!

Unlike most other diesel engines, the governor fitted to the 'Deltic' – of Ardleigh manufacture – was not fed with oil by the main engine driven oil pump, but by its own small Dowty servo pump. This delivered oil to the governor at a pressure of 120lb/sq in and was situated alongside the governor being driven, like most of the engine accessories, by a quill shaft from the main phasing gear case. Sometimes, like the other quill shafts, this one would fail. If it did, this meant a complete engine shut-down, but more usually, failing during the engine starting procedure, the engine would not start. An associated relief valve also relieved at too low a pressure on occasions, and this would have the same result.

The governor itself was regulated by air pressure – known as

regulating air – and this came via a pressure controller situated under, and controlled by, the driver's master controller. Actually each controller had two 'Clayton Dewandre' air control valves, one for each engine, and these would vary the pressure seen by the governor in the range 0–50lb/sq in corresponding to minimum and maximum engine speed, and thus power output. Obviously, it was important that the two valves connected to the respective controllers were sychronised, otherwise the two power units would be out of step with each other. Setting them correctly was a tricky operation. Each governor had an actuator bellows unit, this responded to the air pressure from the controller and in turn controlled the speed control pilot valve. A burst bellows caused an immediate loss of power on the engine in question, the amount of loss depending on how bad was the burst, in any event it would gradually get worse; this fault was not unknown but easily repaired once identified. The complete renewal of the governor, not a frequent occurrence but one occasionally necessary at a depot, was yet another tricky operation. At Finsbury Park we had one or two supervisors and artisans who were specially skilled in the intricate adjustments needed to 'tune' a replacement governor to an engine, and keep the two engines as near in step with each other as possible.

Despite what I have said earlier about the limited work which depots could effectively undertake on the engines in situ, they did over the years develop the necessary skills to carry out a number of jobs more usually considered 'works only'. For example, occasionally a cam-box joint would burst, this was the large casting that contained the fuel pump cam-shaft which was driven from the main gear train in the phasing gear case, and on top of which were the six fuel pumps for whichever bank the cam-box served. Obviously there were three of these cam-boxes, one for each cylinder bank, and a leaking joint would gradually get worse, and have to be attended to. Depots could do nothing with the boxes on 'A' and 'C' banks of the engine, but they could renew the joint on the 'B' bank box as this was the one on top of the engine. Fortunately, in my experience, it was the one that was usually in trouble! It was a tricky operation afterwards to set all the fuel pumps correctly.

The crankshaft dampers occasionally came loose from the shafts themselves, these were viscous filled and by being mounted on the free end of each crankshaft limited the torsional vibration. In the case of the dampers on 'AB' and 'BC' crankshafts, the two at the upper points of the triangle, then if we cold catch them in time, before they became too loose and caused other damage, then we could re-fix them; it was not an easy job, but it would keep another locomotive out of Doncaster Works and thus reduce time out of traffic. There were further odd jobs, but I think I have mentioned enough to illustrate how the depots improved their ability over the years, and helped to give the fleet such a high availability.

The radiator fan gearboxes, of which there were two per engine, a primary which took the drive from the main phasing gear case to No 2 fan, and a secondary which took its drive from the primary and drove No 1 fan, sometimes gave trouble. Usually this consisted of failed bearings or slipping clutches. The centrifugal clutch on the primary box allowed the fans to keep running and loose momentum naturally after the engine stopped. If they slipped, it very often resulted in high coolant temperature on the engine concerned. We could renew the clutch shoes ourselves, but gearbox bearings necessitated replacement of the box, which in turn needed removal of the fan and complete roof section. Spare gearboxes

were few and far between so we did not keep a stock at depots, but Doncaster could usually be relied upon to put one on a passenger train, even if we did have to send a small platoon to King's Cross to collect it!

It always amazed me that the fan drive propeller shafts lasted as long as they did; there were two of these per engine, one from phasing gearbox to primary fan gearbox, and another to the secondary. The universal couplings, two per shaft, took a terrific hammering and lubrication of them, together with examination of their coupling bolts, constituted an important part of every examination. If the coupling on the primary shaft where it coupled to the phasing gear case output came adrift, as it sometimes did, it could do considerable damage while it was flying around loosing momentum. It usually knocked off the overspeed unit and its associated 'Martonair' trip assembly, as well as damaging the engine governor and its linkage. But generally, as I have already indicated, in view of the work these shafts did, troubles were few, provided they had the laid down maintenance.

The use of Ethelyne-Glycol as a coolant inhibitor presented problems at depots because, as well as its high cost, it contaminated drains, being a 'notifiable waste'. Obviously, if an engine had to be drained for any reason, we could not dispose of the coolant, both on grounds of cost, and the drainage problem. So it was necessary to drain it into a suitable receptacle and put it back into the engine after whatever work being undertaken was complete. This was a time-consuming process. Of course, as anybody who does their own car maintenance will know, glycol is extremely 'searching' in a coolant system and if the engines were allowed to stand for long periods, they had a habit of loosing large quantities of coolant through small leaks at the various hose pipe connections.

Towards the end of the locomotives' lives we were able to add a little colour to those allocated to Finsbury Park by painting the cab window surrounds white. This proved quite popular with the public and staff alike. It enabled a depot to be identified with its locomotives and helped boost staff moral during difficult times. It is perhaps worth recalling the problems we encountered with the first locomotive to have the white window surrounds this being No 55.003 in April 1979. We soon found that it was not the easy job we expected, because the body shape of the 'Deltic' gave strange optical illusions if the line of white paint along the roof ran parallel, as one would expect it to, with the cant rail. We found that it had to taper away from the cant rail towards the centre of the locomotive, so as to 'look correct'. It took all the ingenuity of 'Speedy' the painter, and one or two others to overcome this one!

Later on we painted No 55.015 in a similar way for her attendance at the Stratford Depot open day, and afterwards the remainder of the depot's allocation were treated similarly. When the other members of the class were all concentrated at York, that depot placed the City of York's coat of arms alongside the number at each end of their locomotives. Thus, whether they be allocated to Finsbury Park or York, they could be identified, and not only by their names and numbers.

We came through some difficult times whilst I was at Finsbury Park, with the gradual reduction in workload as the Great Northern suburban electrification was inaugurated and then with the coming of the HSTs. When the 'Passenger Loco' closed, all the servicing of locomotives was concentrated at Finsbury Park, 'Deltics' included, and the depot was able to manage with this increase in its throughput. However, we did leave some staff at King's Cross station as 'trouble shooters' and extremely worthwhile they have proved to be. I left the depot myself with a host of happy memories because it was a depot that always gave me a lot of pride. Perhaps this was because it was the first depot I had managed, it is difficult to say. I was proud of its staff and its locomotives and I feel sure its efforts will go down in history; certainly I shall never forget my time their and I shall always look back on it with great affection.

*Left:*
**Looking down on Finsbury Park Depot from the top of the fuel tanks sees an impressive line up of 'Deltics', from left to right: Nos 55.014** *The Duke of Wellington's Regiment* **just leaving the depot, 55.015** *Tulyar,* **55.012** *Crepello* **and 55.009** *Alycidon.* **No 55.012 had been withdrawn that day and was awaiting to make its final journey for scrapping – 20 May 1981** *Gavin Morrison*

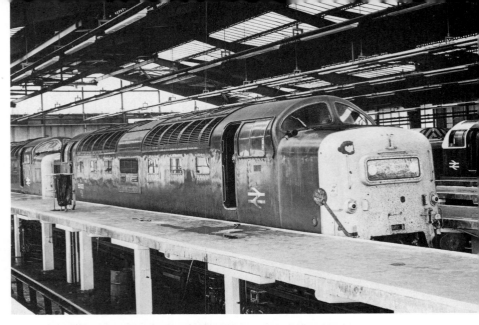

*Right:*
A view taken inside Finsbury Park Depot on
20 May 1981 sees No 55.022 *Royal Scots Grey*
receiving attention, with Nos 55.008 *The Green
Howards* behind and 55.009 *Alycidon* to the
right. *Gavin Morrison*

*Below right:*
Another view inside Finsbury Park Depot, but this
time on 19 September 1980 when No 55.002 *The
King's Own Yorkshire Light Infantry* was being
serviced. No 55.018 *Ballymoss* is under
examination to the right. The two pipes on the
buffer beam to the left of the vacuum brake pipe,
itself to the left of the screw coupling, are the
exhaust pipes from the vacuum exhausters which
were located in No 1 nose end; this was one of the
few external ways of identifying one end from the
other on a 'Deltic'. *Gavin Morrison*

*Bottom right:*
This must be a unique photograph of any depot
because it shows every Manager and every Chief
Maintenance Foreman (later designated Traction
Maintenance Engineer) that Finsbury Park Depot
ever had, along with one or two others connected
with the depot. With their current (1985) jobs as
well as the positions they occupied at Finsbury
Park there are, left to right: Peter Townend,
retired – Traction Maintenance Engineer, King's
Cross Division; John Butt, Regional Mechanical &
Electrical Engineer, WR, Depot Manager (4th);
Tom Greaves, Traction & Train Crew Manager,
BRB, Depot Manager (1st); Chris Kinchin-Smith,
Area Maintenance Engineer, Old Oak Common,
Senior Technical Officer; Don Cowan, Traction
Mainenance Engineer, LMR, Depot Manager
(2nd); Dennis Edwards, retired – Depot Manager
(3rd); Alan Englet, Consultant, Transmark, Site
Engineer when Depot built; Stan Pearce, retired –
Traction Maintenance Engineer (5th); Allan Baker,
Area Mechanical & Electrical Engineer, Stratford,
Traction Maintenance Engineer, (4th) and Depot
Manager (6th); Phil Crosby, Mechanical &
Electrical Engineer, North ER, Traction
Maintenance Engineer (3rd); Frank Frith,
Locomotive Engineer ER, Chief Maintenance
Foreman (2nd); Stan Page, deceased, Chief
Maintenance Foreman (1st), Depot Manager (5th).
*Tulyar* provided the backcloth on 15 May 1981,
just a few days before the depot lost its allocation
of main line diesel locomotives.
*British Railways*

*Above left:*
**'Speedy' (C. Consalves) the depot painter gives *Tulyar* the white cab treatment on 15 August 1979.** *Roger Newling-Goode*

*Above right:*
**Meld complete with 'thistle' 'Flying Scotsman' headboard, which by this date normally reposed in the Traction Maintenance Engineer's office before going into York Museum, provides the background for this portrait of John Foster left, one of the Senior**

**Maintenance Supervisors, and Allan Baker at Finsbury Park on Saturday 30 July 1977.** *Gavin Morrison*

*Below:*
**The offical BR photograph of No D9007 *Pinza* when brand new at Finsbury Park Depot. This would have been taken in late June 1961 and well illustrates all the original features, including the plate frame bogies.** *British Railways*

*Above right:*
**Another 'official' taken on delivery to Finsbury Park of the 2nd of the Brush-Sulzer Type 4s (later Class 47), the first 20 of which all went new to this depot and were for long associated with Finsbury Park and the ECML. She is seen alongside No D9020** *Nimbus* **and the illustration would date from late 1962.**
*British Railways*

*Right:*
**Two 'Deltics' side by side at the fueling bay at Finsbury Park on 20 May 1981. No 55.008** *The Green Howards* **is on the left and No 55.022** *Royal Scots Grey* **alongside. Both these two locomotives ran with their indicator panels in the form shown until withdrawal, never having them completely blanked off. One of the engines has just been started on No 55.008.** *Gavin Morrison*

*Below:*
**Class 08 No 08.810 keeps No 55.011** *Royal Northumberland Fusiliers* **company in the yard at Finsbury Park on 30 November 1980.**
*Gavin Morrison*

*Above:*
**King's Cross Passenger Locomotive Yard was extremely cramped, and this is well illustrated in this view of No 55.005 *The Prince of Wales's Own Regiment of Yorkshire* surrounded by Class 47s on 10 July 1976.** *Gavin Morrison*

*Left:*
**The small depot at King's Cross, where the smaller 'A' examinations could be carried out, as well as minor repairs, is seen in this picture on 7 March 1976 when 'Deltic' No 55.012 *Crepello* was inside, and Nos 55.021 *Argyll & Sutherland Highlander* and 55.003 *Meld* await their next turns of duty.**
*Gavin Morrison*

*Above:*
**The complicated layout at King's Cross is again well illustrated in this picture, together with the small servicing shed. A Class 47 arrives at the terminus with an express, and No 55.011 *Royal Northumberland Fusiliers* runs light engine into the depot for servicing. No 55.012 *Crepello* is inside the shed on 7 March 1976.** *Gavin Morrison*

*Right:*
**No 55.015 *Tulyar* is seen here alongside the new breed, an HST unit at King's Cross on 10 June 1980.** *Gavin Morrison*

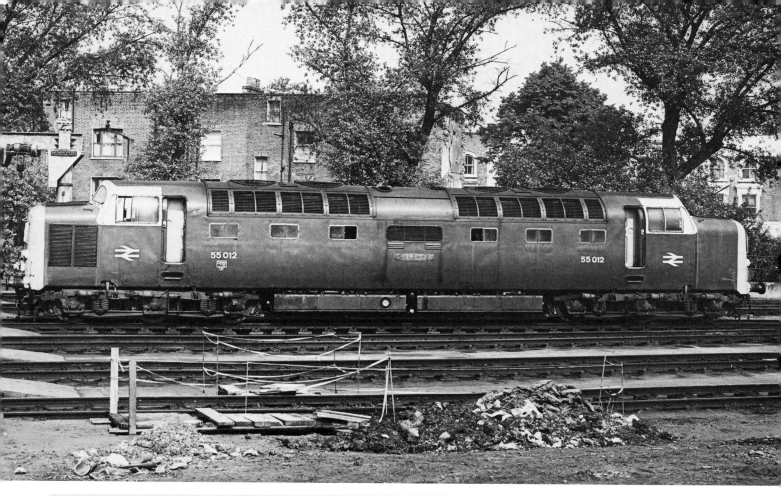

*Above:*
**Wednesday 20 May 1981 was a sad day at the 'Park' as No 55.012 *Crepello* left for its last journey for scrapping. Actually she went first to York depot to have parts removed to keep others running; by this time the sands were fast running out for the fleet. The nameplates have already been removed.** *Gavin Morrison*

*Left:*
**Around mid-day on 20 May 1981 Class 31 No 31.292 arrived to haul No 55.012 to York. Here *Crepello* leaves the 'Park' for the last time.** *Gavin Morrison*

*Right:*
The Finsbury Park football team in front of No 55.015 *Tulyar* on 19 May 1980 and immediately before the locomotive left on her way to the Rainhill celebrations. The team had just won the 'Golden Brake Block' trophy seen, in the twice annual match with rivals Stratford.
*Allan Baker*

*Below:*
No 55.015 *Tulyar* receives attention outside Finsbury Park Depot on 19 September 1980. Two Class 31s together with No 55.022 *Royal Scots Grey* can be seen in the shed.
*Gavin Morrison*

## The Parks' Six White-Cabbed Racehorses

*Right:*
No 55.003 *Meld* is underneath the wires at Carstairs South Junction as she heads south on 4 August 1979 with the 18.25 Edinburgh–Newcastle. This train was diverted during the period that the ECML was blocked after the Penmanshiel tunnel collapse.
*Gavin Morrison*

91

*Above:*
**No 55.009 *Alycidon* accelerates hard past Rossington, just south of Doncaster as she heads the 12.34 Hull–King's Cross on 26 March 1981.**
*Gavin Morrison*

*Right:*
**No 55.009 *Alycidon* approaches Bridge Junction Doncaster with the very last 'Deltic' hauled 14.50 King's Cross–Leeds on 10 April 1981. This train, booked for an HST formation, was frequently 'Deltic' hauled during periods of shortage of the new units, but this was the last time.** *Gavin Morrison*

*Below right:*
**No 55.012 *Crepello* has only another seven weeks of service left when this photograph was taken on 26 March 1981. She is on the slow line south of Doncaster with the 14.10 York–King's Cross semi-fast.**
*Gavin Morrison*

*Above:*
**Tulyar**, No 55.015 is ready to leave Finsbury Park Depot after servicing on 18 September 1980 to work the down 'Hull Executive', 17.05 from King's Cross. *Gavin Morrison*

*Left:*
**Tulyar**, this time complete with the plaque denoting her participation in the Rainhill celebrations leaves Doncaster on the 15.50 York–King's Cross on 17 March 1981. This was the same day that the plaque was unveiled, the locomotive having previously worked the 12.05 King's Cross–York.
*Gavin Morrison*

*Below left:*
No 55.018 **Ballymoss** travelling at around 100mph races down the ECML near Croft on the Edinburgh–Plymouth on 12 November 1981. The 'Deltic' would only be booked to work this train as far as York.
*Gavin Morrison*

*Above right:*
Stainforth Colliery dominates the skyline in this picture of No 55.018 *Ballymoss* as she passes with the 12.34 Hull–King's Cross on 15 April 1981. Notice that the locomotive has numbers at both ends, a feature of the Finsbury Park allocation at this period. *Gavin Morrison*

*Right:*
*Ballymoss* again, this time shunting empty coaching stock for a rail tour just south of Sheffield Midland station on 15 June 1980. The tour was called the 'White Rose'.
*Gavin Morrison*

*Below:*
A comparison of two of the Finsbury Park racehorses with and without the white cabs. No 55.009 *Alycidon* is leaving Edinburgh Waverley for Dunbar during the period when the main line was closed as a through route, whilst No 55.007 *Pinza* is propelling some empty stock out of the station on 4 August 1979. What a difference the white cabs make to the otherwise drab blue livery. *Gavin Morrison*

# 7
# The Second Eleven

As the High Speed Trains (HSTs) were progressively introduced onto the ECML the 'Deltics' got ousted from the top link jobs. But well before this started, indeed as far back as 1973 when the Eastern Region first put in its bid for the 42 HST sets it reckoned it needed to operate the ECML, thoughts had begun to be formulated as to what, if anything, the 'Deltics' could be utilised for afterwards. Much criticism was subsequently levied on the eventual decision to scrap them so early. Especially moreover, as some considerable sums of money had been spent on the HGRs carried out on some of the fleet. However, much thought went into the subject and a number of schemes were considered. There were a few positive offers, but detailed studies put paid to them all, and not without good reason.

I cannot better describe the decision to scrap the 'Deltics' than by quoting a letter I had published in the February 1984 issue of the *Deltic Deadline*, which is the official journal of the Deltic Preservation Society. My letter was in reply to one from a gentleman who had argued long and hard for the class to have been retained for use on another route; he seemed keen on the Midland main line which incidently, had been one of the options considered. I replied:

'If only (the gentleman) realised the thoughts and ideas that went into the decision to scrap the "Deltics" rather than re-deploy them. The financial pressures on BR by the Government over the last few years have been tremendous. The decision to take the class out of traffic at the end of 1981, together with the closure of York depot, were an extremely crucial part of the Eastern Region's budget forecast; to reverse that plan at so late a stage would have jeopardised all number of other schemes that were considerably more fruitful. Yes, the early months of 1982 were extremely difficult over the whole of BR for locomotive availability, but does your correspondent not recall the terrible winter we had, together with the crippling ASLEF strikes? This is why there were locomotives shortages in the diagrams he mentions, not because a dozen or so "Deltics" had been withdrawn. Nobody doubts other depots ability to maintain the locomotives, least of all Toton who have one of the best track records in the country. However, whenever new types of traction are allocated to depots, long experience has taught BR that a 'learning' period of around six – eight months is needed to restore them to whatever availability and reliability they enjoyed before. With the added complexity of the "Deltic", it would not be unreasonable to expect this period to be lengthened to nearer 12 months; a long time for a fleet coming up to 20 years old anyway. We struggled to get 60% availability from the fleet in its later years so your correspondent's 10 locomotives for the Midland main line would only cover about six diagrams; the engines have an extremely limited life between overhauls and one cannot 'rob Peter to pay Paul' with the internal parts of a diesel engine, least of all high speed ones like the "Deltics". I am afraid that my answer to both your correspondent's questions, and I feel I make them after a far more considered approach, is an emphatic No. We have to move with the times, the "Deltics" were a small, highly specialised and expensive fleet, once the prime reason for their existance had disappeared, at 20 years old, they just had to go.'

What this gentleman and others failed to grasp was that it was not just faster schedules the travelling public wanted, but a better environment in which to travel, a new product as we call it today, and the HST is just that. Its image alone was sufficient to get people back to rail travel. When these units were eventually diagrammed for some Midland main lines services the increase in traffic was out of all proportion to the small gains in overall journey times, small because at first they were limited on these services to a maximum speed of 100mph. The 'Deltics' could no doubt have achieved the same, but with older coaches and at a greater cost; the end result would have been a negligible betterment in cash over the booking office counter and at the end of the day, in the harsh world railways have to live in, that is the foremost critera.

We have jumped ahead of the story somewhat, but I was anxious to illustrate that the class were not just scrapped without a lot of thought. To take them away from the Regions and depots that knew them, together with the proximity of the ECML to Doncaster Works, would have been a disaster in view of the period of life left to them, even by the most optimistic withdrawal plan.

As the HSTs started to arrive on the Eastern and Scottish Regions, initially entering traffic in normal locomotive hauled diagrams and schedules, the capabilities of the 'Deltics' became more apparent. Government investment cuts reduced by 10 units the HST order for the ECML, giving a total of 32 sets against a projected 42. Obviously, this set the timetable planners into reverse and many of the services originally envisaged for HST haulage had to retain 'Deltics'. Notable amongst these were the London–Hull trains and one or two seving the West Riding. Additionally, a new series of so-called semi-fast trains intended to serve the intermediate stations like Huntingdon, Grantham, Newark and Retford – along with Stevenage, Peterborough and Doncaster at which some HSTs were to stop too – were to be introduced. There were eight of these services each day, later reduced to seven, and they almost alone of the ECML services were to stop at the stations mentioned – they were an important part of the overall plan and pathing them was difficult. However, by arranging their departures from either King's Cross or York

five minutes behind the hourly HSTs, they could just keep out of the way of the next HST towards the end of their journey. But it needed all the 'Deltics' powers of acceleration and 100mph top speed to complete these runs in the average 2hr and 50min allowed, and this gave an average speed, inclusive of stops, of 66mph. When I was at Finsbury Park my office overlooked the main line and as I watched the 'Deltics' speeding into King's Cross there would generally be an HST hard on their heels. Obviously the Class 47s had neither the accelerative powers nor the top speed and when they were occasionally used on these services, the HST would be right behind them, and delayed, long before the end of the trip. Indeed, the only regular day-time trains the Class 47s continued to be diagrammed to work on the ECML after the introduction of the full HST timetable were those to and from Cleethorpes.

There was still a bright spot in what was left of the Class 55 story as the Hull trains were now to become exclusive to them. To appease Hull's city fathers at their lack of a HST service, the trains serving that city were improved to the hilt of the 'Deltics' power. The principal up and down trains, the 07.00 ex Hull and the 17.05 return from London, which already carried the name the 'Hull Executive', having formerly been a pullman car train – the 'Hull Pullman' – were given extremely fast schedules from the introduction of the May 1979 timetable. Moreover, the down train was booked to make its first stop at Retford after an average 91.3mph sprint from King's Cross. It became at a stroke Britain's fastest-ever scheduled locomotive-hauled train – LMR electric locomotives included. It was a splendid way for the class to end their 20 years of intensive use on the prime ECML services. However, the seven extra HST sets eventually agreed put paid to it and on their delivery in late 1980 and early 1981, the Hull trains progressively went over to HST formations, the 'Hull Executive' on 5 January, 1981.

As a part of the natural interest generated by this amazing King's Cross to Retford timing, a special headboard after the style of the standard BR steam version was made. This adorned the 'Deltic' hauling the train during its first week of operation, was used spasmodically thereafter, and as a swansong during the train's last week of locomotive haulage in early 1981. Unfortunately, a Newark stop inserted from October 1979 had spoilt the high-speed timing but nevertheless the train still had to average 87mph King's Cross–Newark.

The locomotives saw out their last years on the King's Cross–York semi-fasts and the Cleethorpes trains in diminishing numbers as successive withdrawals took place. Re-diagramming of the HST sets and some relaxing of schedules enabled Class 47s to keep time and yet still keep out of the way of their faster rivals.

Very much a part of the HST introduction was the future depot policy on the Eastern Region and as a part of the original submission the closure of two locomotive depots was envisaged. Leeds Holbeck was the first casualty losing its allocation in 1978 and being reduced in status for its remaining locomotive servicing commitment. There was no longer any justification for maintaining any of the 'Deltic' fleet in Scotland, although they did retain a number of overnight Anglo-Scottish trains in their workings. Thoughts were given where the remaining locomotives should be allocated, and having the whole fleet at either Finsbury Park or York were two of the alternatives most likely. In the end a compromise was reached with Finsbury Park retaining its eight locomotives together with a fleet of ETH fitted Class 47s, whilst York

would have the remainder of the 'Deltics' loosing its Class 47s at the same time. As the 'Deltics' were gradually phased out of service both these depots would see a reduced commitment, Finsbury Park being reduced in status to that of a servicing and repair depot, and York closed completely.

Once some of the 'Deltics' were allocated away from their original depots, it was of course inevitable that they would stray into pastures new, and although never actually diagrammed away from the ECML and its immediate branches, they did begin to appear on the north-east to Merseyside trains with increasing regularity. More so when one of the class was actually diagrammed to work an Edinburgh to Liverpool train as far as York. Obviously, sooner or later it would just get left on the train at York, and it often did! However, as none of the LMR footplate crews were ever trained to drive 'Deltics' this could only happen on those trains diagrammed throughout for either York or Leeds footplatemen.

I always considered it a little unfair at the Stockton & Darlington Railway celebrations at Sheldon in August 1975 that a 'Deltic' was not included in the cavalcade. There was such a splendid array of ECML motive power ranging from Stirling's single wheeler, Fletcher's 2-4-0 No 910, Ivatt's Atlantic and Gresley's 'A3' and 'A4' Pacifics; the prototype HST brought up the rear. There should have been a 'Deltic' between the last two. However, a 'Deltic' was included in the 'Rail 150' celebrations in May 1980 when the Rainhill trails were commemorated and No 55.015 did the honours.

Early the following year BR agreed to a request by the Deltic Preservation Society to provide commemorative plaques to be mounted on No 55.015 because of its appearance at Rainhill, and there was some discussion as to where on the locomotive they should be fixed. Eventually they were mounted, one at each end, on the redundant route indicator panel and between the two marker lights. This had the added advantage that when the locomotive was scrapped the whole panel could be removed and presented to the Society. We had a small ceremony at Finsbury Park on 17 March, 1981, when Mr Neville Davies, then Divisional Maintenance Engineer Kings's Cross, unveiled the plaques on No 55.015.

I outlined earlier the spare part supply problems that bedeviled the class in later years and these continued. Some locomotives lay at Doncaster for months and even years. As was to be expected, during these long periods of idleness other material was 'robbed' off them, and by late 1979 Nos 55.001 and 55.020 had become little more than hulks. In January the following year it was decided that they should be withdrawn, the first members of the Class 55 to be taken out of service. Neither had turned a wheel under its own power for over a year; others soon followed. But the less intensive utilisation of the class caused a reduction in maintenance costs and a slight increase in availability. Henceforth connecting rods did not 'come out of bed' with quite the same regularity, it was just as well because once the existing spares were used no more would be ordered.

York depot had its problems, but then so would any other depot faced with a new class already 20 years old and one so different and complex in comparison with any other. However, they grappled with the problems well and after a period of learning returned an acceptable performance. But Doncaster Works remained very much the king-pin in the whole maintenance strategy for the class.

It was during these later years that the 'Deltics' became more and more sought after for railtours, and numerous

specials were organised, both by enthusiast bodies and BR themselves. The Kings' Cross Division organised several very successful trips to the Nene Valley Railway near Peterborough, and these must have been unique at the time because once on the private railway, 'Deltic' and preserved steam locomotive exchanged trains for a run up and down the private line. This was followed by a high speed sprint back to London, the outward journey usually being via one or other of the Great Eastern routes by way of March or Cambridge. No 55.002 hauled the first of these specials on the May Day Bank Holiday of 1981, and Nos 55.009 and 55.007 worked subsequent trips.

No 55.002 had been selected to be re-painted in the original two-tone green livery, albeit with full yellow ends, during its last classified repair at Doncaster in late 1980 and this was a prelude to its 'official' preservation. The repaint was paid for by The Friends of The National Railway Museum, so that the locomotive could spend its last twelve months in traffic in the old livery. Indeed this turned out to be the penultimate classified repair undertaken on any 'Deltic', No 55.009 having the distinction of being the last early the following year. Thereafter, only power units would be changed to use up the spare float, or to make one good locomotive out of two as failures occurred. Originally all such engine changes were carried out at Doncaster, but towards the very end Stratford Regional Repair Shop did a few too.

The closure of Finsbury Park was, for a number of reasons, a long drawn-out affair originally envisaged for May 1980 but actually taking place in June the following year, and then it only reduced the depot to a status similar to Leeds Holbeck – complete closure came two years later in October 1983. I was extremely pleased before I left Finsbury Park, and before it ceased to have an allocation, to be able to assemble together all its past Managers and Chief Maintenance Foremen (by this time re-designated Traction Maintenance Engineer) – both of which positions I had occupied myself. This must have been an almost unique occasion for a depot in this country and the distinguised company – alas no longer all with us today – posed alongside No 55.015 to be suitably recorded for posterity. Needless to say, much reminiscence was exchanged over lunch afterwards.

In the last few months of the 'Deltics' service specials were arranged to a number of places and by all number of organisations as well as BR itself. Even such an unlikely place as Oban featured in their travels, when former Haymarket locomotive No 55.021 found herself there on 2 August; moreover the line had to be specially opened for the train as there was no Sunday service to Oban at that time. For my part it was No 55.015's trip to Bournemouth that was the most enjoyable, because the locomotive visited my new depot at Eastleigh for servicing on the way back. I watched her pass through Shawford that morning on her way to Bournemouth, and in the downpour she made a brave sight among the conductor rails!

No 55.015 was chosen again for a special, this time the very last occasion, for she worked the last 'Deltic'-hauled train on BR on its outward leg from King's Cross to Edinburgh on Saturday, 2 January, 1983. The 12-coach train packed with enthusiasts out to savour the last rites was unfortunately composed of 90mph stock, so no records were going to be broken. That is, if one discounts the number of lineside observers! No 55.022 did the honours on the return journey with No 55.009 standing 'pilot' at Newcastle just in case – both organisers and participants were anxious that the train had 'Deltic' haulage for its entire almost 800 miles and it did. On arrival at King's Cross to a battery of cameras and the televison, it only remained for the three locomotives involved to make their way to Doncaster for disposal. However, all three won a reprieve and have been preserved.

York depot did not outlast the 'Deltics' and closed completely coincident with their withdrawal. The Eastern Region's programme for the introduction of HSTs with consequent savings in locomotives and their maintenance facilities was complete.

*Left:*
**No 55.011 *The Royal Northumberland Fusiliers* awaits the right away from under the magnificient roof of Hull station with the 12.34 to King's Cross on 4 February 1981.** *Gavin Morrison*

*Above:*
**The 08.05 from King's Cross headed by No 55.007 *Pinza* passes the serried rows of terraced houses about one mile from the end of its journey at Hull on 1 May 1980.**
*Gavin Morrison*

*Right:*
**Brough station, reduced to two through tracks and one bay is the site of this photograph of No 55.007 *Pinza* leaving with the 12.34 Hull–King's Cross on 24 February 1981.**
*Gavin Morrison*

*Above left:*
**Gilberdyke Junction, formerly Staddlethorpe, sees No 55.017 *The Durham Light Infantry* passing on 19 March 1981 with the 09.34 Hull–King's Cross.** *Gavin Morrison*

*Left:*
**No 55.014 *The Duke of Wellington's Regiment* in dirty external condition, as is its train, leaves Goole on 27 April 1981 with the 16.30 Hull–King's Cross.** *Gavin Morrison*

*Below:*
**Special train for the Hull Kingston Rovers supporters is headed by No 55.019 *Royal Highland Fusilier*, and is seen here leaving Stainforth on 1 May 1981.** *Gavin Morrison*

*Above:*
**Journey's end for No 55.021** *Argyll & Sutherland Highlander* on the 13.05 King's Cross–Cleethorpes, as she waits to propell the stock out of the station ready to form the 17.33 return working on 28 July 1979. *Gavin Morrison*

*Right:*
The 12.00 relief from Scarborough to Glasgow is about to leave in this photograph taken on 2 September 1980 hauled by No 55.011 *The Royal Northumberland Fusiliers.* Notice that the name plate on the locomotive is missing. *Gavin Morrison*

*Below right:*
25 July 1981 sees No 55.004 *Queen's Own Highlander* having worked from King's Cross on the 05.50, being used again almost immediately to power the 14.55 Edinburgh–Aberdeen. Here she is making a smoky exist through Princes Street gardens in the Scottish capital. *Gavin Morrison*

*Above:*
**The 08.55 Edinburgh Waverley–Aberdeen headed by No 55.017 *The Durham Light Infantry* approaches North Queensferry across the Forth Bridge on 20 April 1981.**     *Gavin Morrison*

*Below:*
**Another view of the Forth Bridge, taken from the west side at North Queensferry and showing green liveried No 55.002 *The King's Own Yorkshire Light Infantry* coming off the bridge on 20 April 1981, and heading the 17.00 Edinburgh–Aberdeen.**     *Gavin Morrison*

*Above right:*
**The 12.40 Aberdeen–Edinburgh, which was the return working of the 08.55 in the morning, is seen climbing from Inverkeithing to North Queensferry. No 55.017 *The Durham Light Infantry* is working hard on 20 April 1981.** *Gavin Morrison*

*Right:*
**Holbeck Depot in Leeds lost its allocation of main line locomotives in 1978. In this picture, taken on 10 October 1977, No 55.008 *The Green Howards* comes off the shed and a Class 45 arrives for servicing.** *Gavin Morrison*

*Below:*
**No 55.015 *Tulyar* was the 'Deltic' that represented the fleet at the 150th Anniversary of the Rainhill Trials during the end of May 1980. As can be seen in this picture, the locomotive looked absolutely superb as it posed outside Finsbury Park having been specially prepared on 15 May that year.**
*British Railways*

*Left:*
***Tulyar*** in the sidings at Bold
Colliery after the cavalcade on
**26 May 1980**.   *Gavin Morrison*

*Below:*
**Still looking immaculate, *Tulyar*
is heading home past
Manchester Victoria with the
National Railway Museum
coaches on 28 May 1980. Notice
the burnished buffer faces and
drawgear.**   *Gavin Morrison*

*Above:*
**To commemorate its participation in the Rainhill celebrations BR agreed to a request by the Deltic Preservation Society to attach plaques on the locomotive. A ceremony took place at Finsbury Park Depot on 17 March 1981 and seen here is Neville Davies, then Divisional Maintenance Engineer King's Cross, unveiling the plaque with Allan Baker, Depot Manager, Finsbury Park looking on.**
*British Railways*

*Right:*
**After the event, No 55.015 roars into life prior to working the 12.20 from King's Cross—York.** *Roger Newling-Goode*

*Above:*
The photographer, and co-author, considers this the finest 'Deltic' sight he has ever seen. No 55.015 *Tulyar* approaches Bridge Junction, Doncaster working the 12.20 King's Cross—York on the day that the plaques were unveiled, 17 March 1981. Despite having been dull and rainy in the capital, the sun managed to shine in Yorkshire. *Gavin Morrison*

*Left:*
The end of the 'Deltics' at Finsbury Park finally came on 31 May 1981, and the 16.05 (Sunday) King's Cross—York was the last working by a 'Deltic' off Finsbury Park Depot whilst it still had its allocation. Needless to say, the 'Park' did not let the event go un-noticed and No 55.009 *Alycidon*, complete with special headboard and wreath did the honours. The train is seen here approaching Doncaster.
*Gavin Morrison*

# Trans Pennine Workings

*Right:*
The use of 'Deltics' on the York–Liverpool trains via the old London & North Western trans-Pennine route over Standedge was a terrific bonus to local 'Deltic' enthusiasts. It was incredible the number of enthusiasts who somehow managed to be at the track side around the Huddersfield area each Thursday morning, during the latter part of 1981, to see the 08.49 York–Liverpool, which was regularly used as a test run for the 'Deltic' rostered to work the succeeding Saturday's 'Deltic' rail-tour. The operation of the 'Deltics' on this route commenced as far back as September 1979, when a telephone call to the photographer informed him that the 09.28 Newcastle–Liverpool had departed the former city with No 55.018 *Ballymoss* in charge. Clearly, there was a good chance it would work this train through to Liverpool, which it did and the locomotive is seen here at Liverpool Lime Street on 8 September 1979.
*Gavin Morrison*

*Centre right:*
No 55.015 *Tulyar* with white cab restored by York Depot (originally they had all been repainted blue on transfer to York), as well as a lot of other white paint, is seen here passing Rainhill station with the 13.05 Liverpool–York on 22 October 1981.
*Gavin Morrison*

*Below right:*
No 55.011 *The Royal Northumberland Fusiliers* was not one of the 'Deltics' kept in immaculate external condition for the rail-tours organised in the last three months of the fleets life. Here she is passing Earlstown with the 08.49 York–Liverpool on 27 October 1981.
*Gavin Morrison*

*Above:*
**No white cabs, but with fuel tanks and roof grilles painted silver, No 55.009 *Alycidon* provided yet another livery variation as she passes Eccles on the 13.05 Liverpool–York on 12 November 1981.**
*Gavin Morrison*

*Left:*
**Acclerating hard away from a signal check near Eccles, No 55.002 *The King's Own Yorkshire Light Infantry* nearly obliterates the road works of the M602 motorway construction on 16 October 1981.** *Gavin Morrison*

*Above:*

**No 55.002 again, about to leave Manchester Victoria on 18 October 1981 with the 13.05 Liverpool–York, the seven coach train will not need the assistance of the Class 25 which was acting as the Miles Platting banker.** *Gavin Morrison*

*Right:*

**No 55.011 *The Royal Northumberland Fusilier* passes the signalbox at Miles Platting on 27 October 1981 with the 13.05 Liverpool–York.** *Gavin Morrison*

*Below right:*

**On 22 October 1981 No 55.015 *Tulyar* was being tried on the 13.05 Liverpool–York and she is seen here approaching the site of Diggle station just before entering Standedge tunnel.** *Gavin Morrison*

*Above:*
**The Pennines are not exactly well known for glorious sunny days in December, and by 14.20 on the 3rd of that month in 1981, it was virtually dark as No 55.009 *Alycidon* emerged from the over three mile journey through Standege tunnel.**
*Gavin Morrison*

*Left:*
**One of the many fine viaducts on the Trans-Pennine route is this one, at Milnsbridge, which No 55.011 *The Royal Northumberland Fusilier* is crossing on 28 October 1981 with the 13.05 Liverpool–York.** *Gavin Morrison*

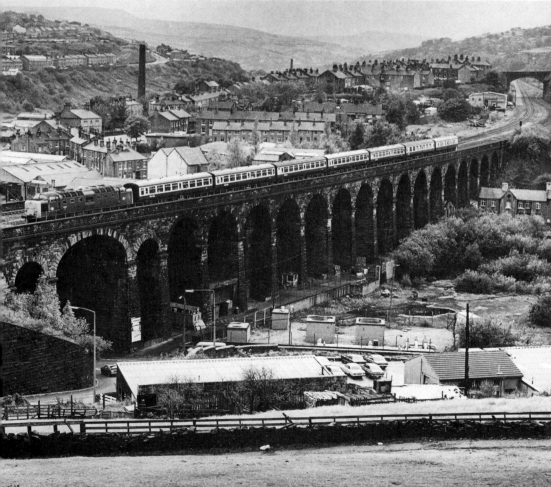

*Above:*
**No 55.011 again, this time emerging into the sunshine from the short tunnel between Springwood Junction and Gledholt to the west of Huddersfield station, with the 08.49 York–Liverpool on 28 October 1981.**
*Gavin Morrison*

*Right:*
**The 13.05 from Liverpool arrives at Huddersfield headed by No 55.004 *Queen's Own Highlander* on 7 September 1980.** *Gavin Morrison*

*Below right:*
**No 55.009 *Alycidon* passes the Calder Valley main line as it approaches Heaton Lodge Junction near Mirfield with the 13.05 from Liverpool–York on 25 November 1981.**
*Gavin Morrison*

*Above:*

**No 55.022 *Royal Scots Grey*
may have been having some
trouble on 4 November 1981,
the Class 45 No 45.005 was
attached at Manchester and
piloted the train through to
York. Perhaps the 'Deltic' only
had one engine operational, or
perhaps it was just to get the
Class 45 to York without a light
engine movement. In any event,
the pair are seen here crossing
Batley viaduct with the 13.05
Liverpool–York.**
*Gavin Morrison*

*Right:*

**Morley tunnel is 1 miles 1,609yd
long and No 55.013 is seen here
emerging from it on the
24 October 1980 with the 13.05
from Liverpool–York.**
*Gavin Morrison*

*Above:*
**The 08.49 from York—Liverpool headed by No 55.011 *The Royal Northumberland Fusiliers*, passes the site of the former LNWR Copley Hill marshalling yards at Leeds on 13 October 1981.** *Gavin Morrison*

*Centre left:*
**The end of the 'Deltics' in BR service finally came on 31 December 1981, when the survivors were sent to Doncaster Works for scrapping. Nearly 12 months after being taken out of service, No 55.004, 55.022, 55.016, 55.005 and 55.017 present a sorry site and they are lined up awaiting the cutting torch. Beyond the line up, and behind the Class 31 is No 55.015. As events were to turn out Nos 55.015, 55.016 and 55.022 were subsequently rescued for preservation.**
*Gavin Morrison*

*Left:*
**Redundant Deltic engines lie rusting in the open at Doncaster Works awaiting disposal on 26 April 1983.** *Gavin Morrison*

# 8
# Preservation

That no less than six 'Deltics' should be preserved is some achievement representing, as it does, slightly over 25% of the fleet. That one should be earmarked for the National Collection was inevitable, but that a further five should be bought privately was not.

The Deltic Preservation Society was one of the first bodies off the mark with a published aim to preserve one locomotive in working order in 1977. As time went on their members thoughts naturally focused on which locomotive should be selected and there was a difference of interests. There were those concerned in getting a locomotive in sound mechanical and electrical condition along with engines in a similar state, and those after their 'own' favourite member of the class. Of course, each member had his own personal favourite. Fortunately the society had a number of experienced advisers who were aware of the problems that would be encountered if the Society wanted actually to run the locomotive, albeit on a preserved line, and in the end their views, which were obviously biased towards a locomotive in sound condition, were adopted. This ensured that one of the locomotives that had had the HGR should be selected, and No 55.016 was the obvious candidate.

Nevertheless, the society decided to carry out a popularity poll among its members via its magazine. Interestingly No 55.015 polled the most votes, even after a second poll, with No 55.009 second. Clearly the 'racehorses' figured high in the enthusiast stakes because no less than seven of them came in the first 10.

As events turned out, No 55.019 was selected rather than No 55.016 and it will be recalled this was the second locomotive to receive an HGR. However, in view of the large amount of money collected by the Society during the last few months that the locomotives were in service, far in excess of that needed to purchase one locomotive, it proved possible to make a bid for two. This was originally partly in lieu of trying to obtain a selection of spares, in that one locomotive could provide a supply for the other, but subsequently as a serviceable locomotive in its own right with the spare parts being obtained separately. It was a magnificent achievement, to collect sufficient money for two complete locomotives and a quantity of spares, to include complete power units, when one considers that only a year before there were doubts whether sufficient money would be available to obtain just one complete locomotive.

Much of the money collected however, particularly towards the end, was for a specific 'Racehorse Fund' on the explicit condition that monies so raised were to be used to help purchase one of the locomotives with a racehorse name, and not to assist with any other aspect of the Society aims. Again there was indecision as to which locomotive should be

tendered for once it was established that sufficient money would be available for two locomotives rather than one. But as No 55.009 had had the very last 'Deltic' classified repair, was still in service to the end and was in reasonably good condition, the choice fell on her.

There were a number of conditions imposed by BR on the sale of 'Deltic' locomotives, and these included surcharges over and above their scrap value if the buyers wanted to retain the cast-steel bogies and train air brake equipment. Readers will recall that the locomotives had been built originally with a plate frame fabricated bogie, and that these were subsequently replaced by cast ones in view of the troubles encountered. The fabricated variety were utilised under the Class 37s as they undertook less arduous work, but they had still given far more trouble over the years and were heavier on maintenance. BR now wanted to take the opportunity of using the cast bogies from withdrawn 'Deltics' to replace the worst of the fabricated bogies from the Class 37s, and whilst they would consider selling cast bogies with 'Deltics' the costs were considered prohibitive to the society; the alternative was a set of fabricated bogies, albeit in fair condition. The train air brake equipment however, was somewhat different and the possibility that one day the locomotives may be allowed to venture out on the main lines, together with the incomplete state the locomotives would be in if this equipment was removed, made up the minds of society members to pay the surcharge to retain this gear. It is perhaps worth pointing out at this juncture that payment of the surcharge was made possible by, among other things, an increase in society finance from donations by no less than £20,000 in the period May 1981 to March 1982.

The two locomotives were handed over to the society by Mr Alan Sourbut, Chief Mechanical & Electrical Engineer Eastern Region, at a small ceremony at Doncaster Works on 20 August, 1982. Mr Sourbut, in accepting the cheque for £33,100 (the actual price paid for the two locomotives was this plus VAT) in payment for Nos 55.009 and 55.019, closed his speech by wishing the society well with their new acquisitions and he hoped 'that all their flashovers would be little ones' – I do too! The two locomotives under the tow of Class 37 No 37.100, left the same day en route to their new home on the North Yorkshire Moors Railway at Grosmont, where they arrived the following day.

I wish this society and its locomotives well, they certainly deserve it. However, they have formidable problems ahead of them keeping such intricate and complicated machinery in working order. This is especially so in view of the comparatively small amount of use it will get. Diesel engines like to be run, and electrical machinery and control gear more so. Nothing can be potentially more damaging to electrical

machines than to be left in damp conditions for long periods, unused for months on end. Problems of this nature have, I believe, already been experienced and I hope that lessons have been learnt and remedies devised to go some way towards alleviating them. In their time on the railway the locomotives have already put in many miles and it is good to know that one or two of the former Finsbury Park and York maintenance staff are regular volunteers who go along and help carry out much of the maintenance and repair work. I believe it is the eventual intention to restore No 55.019 to the original two-tone green livery, and for No 55.009 to retain the all over blue and white cabs.

We have already seen how No 55.002 was selected as the locomotive to be 'officially' preserved and after remaining in traffic to the end of the class life, this locomotive went into York Museum. It had of course already been restored to the original two-tone green livery, albeit with full yellow ends and the TOPS five figure numbering. It has retained this livery since entering the museum and has emerged on a number of occasions to attend BR depot open days and the like.

One could be forgiven for expecting that this would be the end – not so, for no less than three more locomotives have also been saved. However, before any positive moves were made there was a rather bizarre attempt to auction No 55.015 by no less a house than Christie's of London. The abortive event took place on 16 December, 1982 – the locomotive, let me hasten to add, remaining at Doncaster Works – when the bidding rose from an initial £4,000 to £5,500 and, not having reached the reserve price – whatever that was – the locomotive was withdrawn from the sale. A number of 'Deltic' nameplates were however sold. Prices ranged from £950 to £1,100, which princely sum those of *Royal Highland Fusilier* fetched.

Next on the list of locomotives saved was the first of the class, no less than No D9000 itself, by now of course 55.022. Incidently, despite being the first numerically D9000 was not the first to enter traffic, this was No D9001. No D9000 was unfortunately damaged in an accident at the makers Vulcan Foundry just before delivery and, although the damage was slight it was sufficient to allow No D9001 to overtake her on the production line. No 55.022 was purchased by the Deltic 9000 Fund in March 1983 and moved to a new home on the Nene Valley Railway near Peterborough on 8 September that year. Almost immediately however, she left again to attend the BR depot open day at the newly-commissioned Norwich Crown Point Depot; this event taking place on 21 September. But the members of the owning society appear to have put in a lot of work after the locomotive's 18 month sojourn in Doncaster Works yard because, over the weekend of 22–23 October 1983, No 55.022 was in service on the Nene Valley Railway and with both its engines serviceable.

Despite attracting nobody with sufficient funds on auction, No 55.015 was saved by Mr Peter Sanson who purchased the locomotive in February 1984. However, before this took place *Tulyar* had one more task to complete for its original owners

and for which it had been moved to the Railway Technical Centre at Derby. It was realised at the eleventh hour that the basic 100mph track behaviour data then still being used by BR emanated from tests done with the 'Deltic' many years before. There was a requirement to update this to take account of higher top speeds with the HST and APT then in use, and at the same time it was decided that it would be well worthwhile backchecking the original data with the vastly better test equipment then available. Thus No 55.015 participated in static tests at Derby before becoming redundant once more. Being at Derby it was but a short distance to the Midland Railway Centre at Butterley Station, Ripley where No 55.015 is now undergoing restoration; but she needs a lot of work doing on her. One should remember that this locomotive was used as a guinea pig to see how far classified repairs could be extended, and in consequence had little body attention for some years. Nevertheless, as the leader of the Deltic Preservation Society popularity poll, and having often been in the limelight in later years, the locomotive deserves a place in the preservation movement.

Last but by no means least No 55.016 was saved after all, having been the original choice of the Deltic Preservation Society, and having had the most work carried out under the HGR programme. It seems strange she should be the last to be saved, but so be it. The members of The Deltic 9000 Fund originally decided to try to obtain some spare power units, and then turned their attention to a complete locomotive as back-up spares. The purchase was successfully completed in the early months of 1984 and No 55.016, minus train air brake equipment, journeyed south from Doncaster to the Nene Valley Railway on 30 July 1984. This locomotive suffered badly during her long period out of use in Doncaster Works, but who can say that one day we will not hear the roar of the twin Napier Deltics as they spring into life again? Indeed *Gordon Highlander* was due to return to use in late 1984 for operation on the Nene Valley Railway.

In conclusion to this brief chapter, which must be but a prelude to much more being written about these locomotives, I would like to wish those intrepid enthusiasts who have gone to such ends to secure them for preservation the best of luck. I know that they will have their work cut out in years to come, a diesel locomotive is a handful, a 'Deltic' more than most. They will need all the help that they can muster because bitter experience taught BR that 'Deltic' engine problems are always expensive. But the various societies have benefitted from BR experience in that a number of spare power units have been acquired. It was accepted from the inception of the class that the whole maintenance philosophy would be based on regular power unit changes and the wisdom of this was very soon confirmed in practice, not only for maintenance but for repairs too. The reasons for this are twofold, the comparatively short engine life and the almost complete inaccessibility to do anything at all on the engines when in position in a locomotive. Power to their elbows!

## 'Deltic' Wanderings

*Above right:*
Prior to the arrival of the HSTs on the Eastern Region, BR were always reluctant to release 'Deltics' for railtours, but there was the odd relaxation. One such occasion was an RCTS West Riding Branch tour from Leeds to Edinburgh via the Settle & Carlisle and Waverley routes and this was on 5 January 1969, the last day that the Waverley line remained open as a through route. No D9007 *Pinza* was the chosen motive power and she provided some lively running with the nine coach load. Passing Appleby at 70mph she proceeded to cover the 17.5 miles from that point to Ais Gill summit in but 14min, passing Mallerstang Box at 74mph. This was not appreciated by the restaurant car crew, who were attempting to serve the soup with the evening meal at the time! *Pinza* is seen here at Riccarton during a photo stop and she had been well turned out for this historic occasion by Finsbury Park.
*Gavin Morrison*

*Right:*
Haymarket's No 55.022 *Royal Scots Grey* looking extremely well turned out for the 'Deltic Pioneer' tour, seen here entering Bolton on 7 October 1979. This tour continued to Preston and then the WCML to Carlisle and across to Newcastle.    *Gavin Morrison*

*Below right:*
The 'Deltic Ranger' railtour had been scheduled to visit the West Country, but severe weather caused it to be terminated at Bristol Temple Meads on 19 February 1978. No 55.018 *Ballymoss* is seen here running round her train at Bristol, the first occasion one of the class had visited that city.
*J. A. M. Vaughan*

*Above left:*
**Sheffield Midland had a visit from *Ballymoss* too, here No 55.018 is seen with the 'White Rose' railtour, well turned out by Finsbury Park on 15 June 1980.** *Gavin Morrison*

*Left:*
**On 23 July 1978 the Sheffield area of BR ran a special from Chesterfield to Carlisle with No 55.003 *Meld*. The route was via Barnsley to Wakefield, and then via Normanton to Leeds. The train is seen here at Horbury Junction joining the former Lancashire & Yorkshire line at the point where the M1 motorway crosses over the railway.** *Gavin Morrison*

*Below:*
**The 'Deltics' made occasional appearances on specials over the Settle & Carlisle route and at least eight members of the class are known to have worked over it. On 14 November 1981 No 55.009 *Alycidon* headed the 'Deltic Cumbrian' and is seen here passing the closed Ais Gill signalbox.** *Gavin Morrison*

*Above:*
**Alycidon** again, and on the same trip, this time seen passing the closed signalbox at Dent where a stop was made for photographs. *Gavin Morrison*

*Right:*
**No 55.013 The Black Watch** is storming up Beattock Bank near Greskine in the early morning light of 5 May 1980 with the diverted 22.30 (Saturday) King's Cross–Edinburgh. The 'Deltics' only just carried enough fuel to complete the London–Scotland journey via Carlisle after their water capacity had been increased at the expense of fuel. *Gavin Morrison*

*Below right:*
**No 55.003 Meld** is seen here returning from Carlisle to Chesterfield with a BR organised special from the Sheffield area. The 13-coach train sparkles in the evening sun as it passes Holbeck depot at Leeds. The viaduct in the background carries a route more familiar to this class of locomotive, being the main line to Doncaster from Leeds. The date is 23 July 1978.
*Gavin Morrison*

*Above:*
**Having failed to reach the West Country on 19 February 1979 due to severe weather conditions, the 'Deltic Ranger' tried again and, as can be seen here, succeeded on 5 March. This time No 55.005 *Meld* provided the power and she is seen passing along the warren at Dawlish.** *A. Smith*

*Above left:*
**Several tours were run in 1981 from London, over various Great Eastern routes, and onto the Nene Valley Railway at Peterborough. On each occasion the 'Deltic' worked its train over the private line, and then did a further trip with some of the preserved rolling stock. Here can be seen No 55.007 *Pinza* on 12 September with some of the Nene Valley coaching stock.**
*Gavin Morrison*

*Left:*
**BR organised two 'Deltic' tours from Newcastle to Whitby with No 55.002 *The King's Own Yorkshire Light Infantry*. On 2 August 1981 the train is approaching Middlesbrough with the Newport lifting road bridge over the River Tees dominating the skyline.**
*Gavin Morrison*

119

*Above:*
**A fine view of Whitby is obtained from the new road bridge, showing the Abbey and harbour to advantage. On this occasion, 2 August 1981, No 55.002 is returning to Newcastle in the evening sunshine.** *Gavin Morrison*

*Right:*
**No 55.015 *Tulyar* in immaculate external condition, and complete with 'Hull Executive' headboard, is the centre attraction at Stratford Depot open day on 7 July 1979; look at the queue to visit her footplate.** *British Railways*

*Above:*
A familiar scene when 'Deltics' were on railtour duties was the crowds, seen here to advantage. No 55.018 *Ballymoss* is the centre of their attention on this occasion as she poses for the cameras at Cardiff with an RPPR special from Paddington to Treherbert on 29 January 1978.
*M. Rhodes*

*Left:*
Just over a year before No 55.002 *The King's Own Yorkshire Light Infantry* was withdrawn, it entered traffic after overhaul restored to the original two-tone green livery. The cost was borne by the Friends of the National Railway Museum, and a dedication ceremony was held at the museum. The scene is shown here on 12 December 1980, and later in the day the locomotive hauled the 14.15 train from York to London.    *Gavin Morrison*

*Right:*

A sight to gladden the hearts of 'Deltic' enthusiasts, No 9000 *Royal Scots Grey* roars into life, 21 months after withdrawal from normal service, and prior to being handed over to the Deltic 9000 Limited preservation group in Doncaster Works Yard on 7 September 1983. The locomotive had some work carried out on it prior to sale, and is now based on the Nene Valley Railway.
*Gavin Morrison*

*Below:*

The Deltic Preservation Society owns two 'Deltics', Nos 55.009 *Alycidon* and 55.019 *Royal Highland Fusilier*, and they chose the extremely scenic North Yorkshire Moors Railway as their base. No 55.019, in standard BR blue livery makes a fine sight at Green End on 2 July 1983, working the 10.55 Grosmont–Pickering. Currently the society are building a shed for the locomotive.
*P. J. Robinson*

*Above left:*
The magnificent scenery of the North Yorkshire Moors line is well illustrated in this photograph of No 55.009 *Alycidon* in Finsbury Park livery of blue with white cabs and numbers at each end. She is seen here heading through Newtondale with the 11.55 Grosmont–Pickering on 11 August 1984.　*P. J. Robinson*

*Above right:*
A sight that at the end of 1981 was only a dream for 'Deltic' enthusiasts. The Deltic Preservation Society's two locomotives, here carefully positioned for a photograph at Grosmont on the

North Yorkshire Moors Railway. *Alycidon* on the left, and *Royal Highland Fusilier* heading a special on 16 April 1983, is on the right.　*A. P. Haighton*

*Below:*
Prior to being bought for preservation No 55.016 *Gordon Highlander* and 55.015 *Tulyar* make a sorry sight at the back of Doncaster Works on 26 April 1983. The former has now joined No 9000 *Royal Scots Grey* on the Nene Valley Railway and *Tulyar* has moved to Butterley.　*Gavin Morrison*

# 9
# In Retrospect

Having looked at the 'Deltics' from the inception of the prototype, and dealt in some detail with their achievements and maintenance problems, it is opportune to look at them retrospectively in the overall BR traction policy and modernisation plans. Was it all worth it one might ask?

Diesel traction of the main line railways of this country can be said, for all intents and purposes, to have commenced with the introduction of diesel-electric shunting locomotives on the LMS in prewar days. With one or two exceptions the production examples all used an engine from the already proven English Electric 'K' range. This engine has its origins in development work carried out by Messrs William Beardmore of Glasgow and Willans & Robinson of Rugby. Design staff from Beardmore's made redundant in the post World War 1 slump, migrated to Rugby and continued their work, combining it with some development work on diesel engines done by Willans & Robinson earlier. In late 1918 this company had become one of the constituents of the English Electric Co Ltd, and the 'K' range of diesel engines was introduced.

The actual engine used in the locomotives was designated the 6KT, the T indicating traction, and starting life in 1934 rated at 300bhp it was very soon up-rated to deliver 350bhp. It was a six cylinder, vertical in-line four stroke featuring cast iron components and separate cylinder heads; large, heavy and lazy, it developed its rated output with commensurate ease. Indeed, in the last orders for shunting locomotives in the 1960s it was slightly uprated to delivery 400bhp. In turbo-blown form the same engine is capable of over 1,000bhp, and this gives some idea of how under-rated it is in the standard BR shunter. It is of course, this low rating that gained it such a reputation for reliability and low maintenance costs, together with an almost endless life. To a large extent, the success of the diesel shunters with this engine prompted an extension of diesel rail traction by the LMS in this country.

English Electric made the next move, in trying to obtain a foothold in the expanding export market for diesel engined locomotives, they used the 'K' range principles in the design and development of larger engines. Thus, the classic 'K' 10in × 12in cylinder bore and stroke and the main design features were promulgated into a 'V' form turbo-charged engine which, with 16 cylinders – eight per bank – and rated at 1,600bhp, went into the postwar twin LMS main line diesel-electrics Nos 10000 & 10001. Later, slightly up-rated to deliver 1,750bhp, the same engine was used by the Southern Railway for their two locomotives 10201 and 10202, although neither saw service until well into BR days. Later still, with bigger turbo blowers, a four instead of a two-valve cylinder head, and running 100rpm faster at 850rpm, the same basic engine delivered 2,000bhp and powered the third of the Southern-inspired trio, No 10203. Subsequently, it was used in the

English Electric Type 4, later Class 40 and, apart from the 'Deltics', derivatives of it found their way into all other English Electric engined locomotives built for BR.

At 2,000bhp it is an extremely reliable engine, but large and heavy by some standards and still well below its possible rating. However, compared with other engines of similar ratings it has a low wear rate and light maintenance requirement. The early main line diesels were an undoubted success, but they operated on a 'steam railway', sharing steam's working diagrams, with the large time allowances for the essential daily servicing required by steam locomotives. They also had to share the steam maintenance facilities and depots; it was therefore, not unnatural to expect that their performance would improve with purpose-built facilities. What was perhaps not fully realised, was the more extensive diagramming, and therefore higher utilisation, that would become possible when whole fleets were available, rather than just odd locomotives, and the resultant high levels of maintenance and repair. But their high capital cost, when compared with steam, made more extensive use essential. So BR headed for extensive dieselisation, on a massive scale by any standards, and with experience confined to small shunting locomotives and a handful of main line prototypes that had never had the opportunity of being fully extended, either in performance or utilisation.

The majority of the early diesel-electric locomotives introduced by BR employed engines on the same principles as the English Electric; four-stroke and medium speed. The most notable exeptions were the Crossley engined Metropolitan-Vickers Co-Bos which had an eight-cylinder two-stroke rated at 1,200bhp, and the 'Deltics'. The diesel-hydraulic locomotives which were introduced on the Western Region employed small high speed engines and in consequence were much lighter and had more power available for traction. These locomotives gained some success and their light weight was a distinct advantage over the much heavier diesel-electrics, which point did not go unnoticed in some circles. Most of the hydraulic classes used two engines, not least because the size and disposition of the transmission units on a twin-bogied locomotive lends itself to that concept. But still, the two high speed engines were lighter than one medium speed one. The success of the prototype 'Deltic' led BR and English Electric to agree on the use of Deltic engines in a small batch of Bo-Bo diesel-electrics as a part of the evaluation process. On this occasion the 9-cylinder engine was used, turbo-blown and rated at 1,100bhp, the resultant locomotives, somewhat naturally known as the 'Baby-Deltics', falling into the power category Type 2. Unfortunately, right from their entry into traffic in mid-1959 these locomotives were plagued with problems and were a constant source of trouble and anxiety,

almost always with the engine or auxiliaries. Indeed, so bad was their reputation on the Great Northern suburban services, on which they had been allocated since delivery, that by 1962 the whole class had been withdrawn from service and stored. Whatever effect this might have had on the subsequent order for their big sisters had they not already been ordered is academic, it was too late.

The later history of the 'Baby Deltics' need not detain us long, suffice it to say that eventually they were completely refurbished by their makers and many of their troublesome components modified. They re-entered service in 1964 and survived until a general reduction in the BR locomotive fleet size made them redundant, when they were finally withdrawn between 1968 and 1971; being such a small class they had little chance of survival in any such exercise.

The principle of two high speed and low-weight engines used on the hydraulic classes offered great advantages; if this could be adopted on a diesel-electric, without the hydraulic transmission problems being experienced, then perhaps this was the answer to the problem of getting a high power diesel-electric. Indeed the prototype 'Deltic' had already proved it; otherwise, the 2,750bhp of the later Class 47 was all that was even on the drawing board. But like the early mainline diesels, the prototype 'Deltic' had never been extended in service or diagrammed anywhere near its theoretical capacity. Nevertheless the production 'Deltics' were ordered and to a very large extent did what was expected and required of them, but at a cost.

Apart from the Western Region, BR did not generally equip itself to carry out major repairs or component changes at the new depots; reliance was to be placed on the main workshops to perform this function. Thus, when it became evident for instance, that traction motor life on some classes was nowhere near that expected, the necessary facilities had to be provided. To a large extent this was understandable, because nobody really knew what diesel maintenance was all about. The Western Region of course, in going for the high speed engines, anticipated a shorter life and its depots had the facilities to exchange engines and transmission units.

So the 'Deltics' arrived on Regions geared to a policy of allowing main works to carry out major component changes and they, more than any other diesel-electric, would have benefitted from a maintenance philosophy similar to that of the Western Region. Doncaster Works became the king-pin and without in any way undermining what it achieved over the years, if the depots had been able to undertake engine changes, not only to fit an exchange unit, but also to carry out repairs to otherwise inaccessible parts, costs might have been reduced and availability improved.

The 'Deltics' cost £22,000 more per locomotive than, for example a Class 40, so was it worth it? It is difficult to estimate how much traffic the Deltics were able to keep on rail by the standards they achieved. If it had taken half an hour longer to get from London to Scotland in the 1970s how much traffic would the railways have lost? We can only take the word of the commercial boys who said it was significant. That there was nothing else on the market in 1958 to equal the Deltics is an undeniable fact.

In May 1962 English Electric placed into traction service the latest version of the 16 cylinder engine used in Nos 10000 & 10001, and with bigger turbo-blowers and charge-air cooling this developed 2,700bhp. Fitted into a Deltic bodyshell and numbered DP2 (Diesel prototype 2 – the prototype 'Deltic' had been DP1) it was a remarkable locomotive. After initial trials on the LMR, DP2 was transferred to the Eastern Region at Finsbury Park where it worked turn and turn about with the Deltics. Indeed, interestingly it substituted for them as they were successively returned to their makers for modifications, in particular to the train heating boilers.

On this work DP2 did well, and during 58 consecutive days in 1963 achieved a total of 43,000 trouble free miles, proving itself master of the 'Deltic' diagrams. Whether it could have kept pace with the subsequent accelerations to the schedules over the next 10 years must remain a matter for speculation, but one is left wondering, because if it could, it would have done so at a far less cost. The success of DP2, which was itself unfortunately damaged beyond economic repair in an accident at Thirsk in July 1967, led to the BR order for the Class 50 locomotives. DP2 incidentally, remained English Electric property until its end.

But whatever 22 DP2s might or might not have been able to achieve had they been available rather than the 'Deltics', they were not to be. It was 1958 when the 'Deltics' were ordered, and DP2s would not have been available for production until 1963. So, to my mind BR was right to press for the 'Deltics' when it did; it was unfortunate that they were so late in delivery. Should it have been possible to replace them in around 1972, and a 10–12 year life for main line diesel locomotives was predicted when they were ordered, that there is little doubt that 22 locomotives like DP2 would have done the job, and at less cost. But like all nationalised industries, our railways have to answer to the government of the day, and such investment is not always possible, so it was right to keep the 'Deltics' running until the HSTs came along to replace them. As Peter Townend tells us in his Foreword, by the late 1970s the sands were running out for conventional locomotives on fast passenger trains. Even at 100tons on six axles, weight was a problem if speeds were to increase over the 100mph mark, otherwise the additional cost of track maintenance was considerable. The answer had to be division of the power, and this is how the fixed formation train sets of the HST era came about and with these, by dividing the power between the two separate power cars, axle loadings were reduced significantly, and hence so were track maintenance costs.

We shall never really know if the books balanced at the end of the day, any more with the 'Deltics' than other individual types of traction. But they were magnificent locomotives and, perhaps among the the only ones in this age to come anywhere near capturing the magic of their forebearers, and what better line of railway exists anywhere in the world for them to have shown their paces? I salute them for what they were, masterpieces of the locomotive engineer's and diesel engine manufacturer's arts, for which this country is so famous and of which in the 'Deltics' it can be so justly proud.

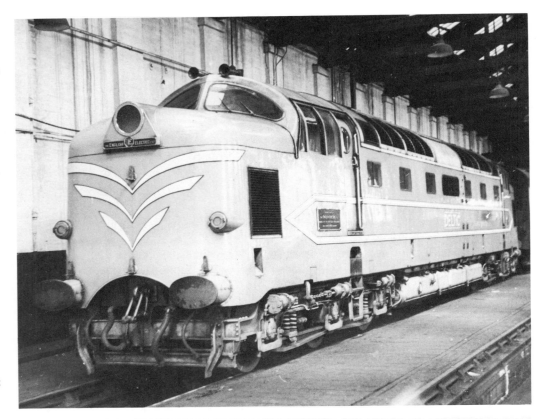

*Right:*
**The prototype 'Blue Deltic' inside Carlisle Kingmoor Motive Power Depot complete with one of the former LMS mobile testing units, resting between test runs over the Settle & Carlisle route on 16 September 1957.** *B. Stubbings*

*Below:*
**No D9012 *Crepello* makes a fine sight in its two tone green livery as she approaches Leeds Central on the down 'West Riding' early in 1962**
*British Railways*
*Brian Webb collection*

*Far right:*
**No 55.003 *Meld* makes an impressive departure from King's Cross with the inaugural accelerated 'Hull Executive' on the first day of its record-breaking timing to Retford on 14 May 1979. This train was booked to average 91.3mph on that journey, the fastest locomotive-hauled train in the country, and a fine achievement for the 'Deltics' in their twilight years.** *Roger Newling-Goode*

*Above, right:*
**The beginning and the end for No D9004/55.004. She is seen when only 5 months old inside the fuelling shed at her home depot of Haymarket, on 14 October 1961, and at Doncaster Works 14 months after withdrawal, awaiting the cutting torch on 9 December 1982.** *K. M. Falconer, Gavin Morrison*

*Below:*
**The end of the line for No 55.013** *The Black Watch* **on 9 December 1982, in the scrap roads at Doncaster Works.**
*Gavin Morrison*

# Appendices

## 1 Diagrams

Illustrated here is a complete set of the original cyclic diagrams introduced after the whole fleet was delivered covering the perod 18 June–9 September 1962; the first Summer in which all members of the class were available. It will be seen that each locomotive has a full week's work, this being quite an innovation at the time, and there is no allowance for any of the fleet being in main works. However, it should be added that some of the other Eastern Region diesel types – notably Class 40 and 45 – had similar full week diagrams at this time. It will also be seen that the North Eastern and Scottish Regions (ie Gateshead and Haymarket) made different provision for depot maintenance than did the Eastern Region, and I have already made mention of this in Chapter 3. It very soon became clear that to diagram locomotive maintenance in this way was not successful, and many were the pit-falls. Later policy was to diagram locomotives for shorter periods, around 24hr at the most, and allow in the fleet totals more locomotives than diagrams, the resulting additional locomotives becoming the 'maintenance spares'.

Diagramming locomotives is a subject of great complexity, and much ingenuity is needed to get the best out of them. I hope that these representative examples will provide material for study because they are well worth it. They show the clever use of power by experienced people and the method of marrying trains to locomotives and vice versa. They should also illustrate how accurate the engineer has to be with his projected availability figures, because the timetable and diagrams are built around them and they have to be achievable day in and day out. If the figure is too low he will be accused of having a fleet of too many locomotives, and if it is too high, commitments will not be met and trains will have to be cancelled. A tightrope to walk!

**Main line diesel locomotive diagrams**
**Eastern Region: King's Cross**

**Locomotive Diagram KX1**

| Arrive | | | Depart |
|---|---|---|---|
| **Sunday** | | | |
| | Shed | ... ... ... ... ... | 10 0pm |
| — | King's Cross | ... ... ... ... ... | 10 30pm |
| **Monday** | | | |
| 12 29am | Grantham | ... ... ... ... ... | 12 37am |
| 2 7am | York | ... ... ... ... ... | 2 17am |
| 3 49am | Newcastle | ... ... ... ... ... | 3 50am |
| 4 0am | Gateshead Shed (Fuel and Insp) | ... ... ... ... | |
| | Gateshead Shed | ... ... ... ... ... | 9 25am |
| — | Newcastle | ... ... ... ... ... | 9 40am |
| 2 28pm | King's Cross | ... ... ... ... ... | — |
| — | Shed (Fuel) | ... ... ... ... ... | 4 55pm |
| — | King's Cross | ... ... ... ... ... | 5 25pm |
| 8 40pm | Leeds Central | ... ... ... ... ... | 10 0pm |
| **Tuesday** | | | |
| 3 25am | King's Cross | | — |
| — | Finsbury Park MD (Maintenance) | ... ... ... ... | |
| | Finsbury Park MD | ... ... ... ... | 3 0pm |
| — | King's Cross | ... ... ... ... ... | 4 0pm |
| 8 1pm | Newcastle | ... ... ... ... ... | 8 4pm |
| 10 0pm | Edinburgh (Fuel and Insp) | ... ... ... ... ...' | — |
| | Haymarket Shed | ... ... ... ... ... | 11 10pm |
| | Edinburgh | ... ... ... ... ... | 11 50pm |
| **Wednesday** | | | |
| 2 12am | Newcastle | ... ... ... ... ... | 2 20am |
| 7 33am | King's Cross | ... ... ... ... ... | — |
| — | Shed (Fuel) | ... ... ... ... ... | 9 30am |
| — | King's Cross | ... ... ... ... ... | 10 0am |
| 2 1pm | Newcastle | ... ... ... ... ... | 2 4pm |
| 4 0am | Edinburgh | ... ... ... ... ... | — |
| — | Haymarket Shed (Fuel and Insp) | ... ... ... ... | |
| | Haymarket Shed | ... ... ... ... ... | 9 21pm |
| — | Edinburgh | ... ... ... ... ... | 10 1pm |
| **Thursday** | | | |
| 12 9am | Newcastle | ... ... ... ... ... | 12 11am |
| 5 28pm | Holloway CLB | ... ... ... ... ... | — |
| — | Shed (Fuel) | ... ... ... ... | |
| | Shed | ... ... ... ... ... | 7 30am |
| | King's Cross | ... ... ... ... ... | 8 0am |
| 12 16pm | Newcastle | ... ... ... ... ... | 12 19pm |
| 2 19am | Edinburgh | ... ... ... ... ... | — |
| — | Haymarket Shed (Fuel) | ... ... ... ... | |
| | Haymarket Shed | ... ... ... ... ... | 3 20pm |
| — | Edinburgh | ... ... ... ... ... | 4 0pm |
| 5 55pm | Newcastle | ... ... ... ... ... | 5 58pm |
| 10 0pm | King's Cross | ... ... ... ... ... | — |
| — | Shed (Fuel and Insp) | ... ... ... ... | |
| | **Stand Pilot 10 30pm to 4 30pm** | | |
| **Friday** | | | |
| | Shed | ... ... ... ... ... | 4 55pm |
| — | King's Cross | ... ... ... ... ... | 5 25pm |
| 8 40pm | Leeds Central | ... ... ... ... ... | 10 0pm |
| **Saturday** | | | |
| 1 2am | Grantham | ... ... ... ... ... | 1 12am |

| Arrive | | Depart |
|---|---|---|
| 3 25am | King's Cross | — |
| — | Shed (Fuel) | |
| — | Shed | 9 5am |
| — | King's Cross | 9 35am |
| 2 4pm | Newcastle | 2 5pm |
| 2 15pm | Gateshead Shed (Fuel) | — |
| — | Gateshead Shed | 8 5pm |
| — | Newcastle | 8 20pm |
| 9 54pm | York | 10 10pm |
| **Sunday** | | |
| 12 44am | Grantham | — |
| 3 0am | King's Cross | — |
| — | Shed (Fuel and Insp) | |
| — | Shed | 9 30am |
| — | King's Cross | 10 0am |
| 5 39pm | Edinburgh | |
| — | Haymarket Shed (Fuel and Insp) | |
| — | Haymarket Shed | 9 32pm |
| — | Edinburgh | 10 1pm |
| **Monday** | | |
| 12 9am | Newcastle | 12 11am |
| 5 28pm | Holloway CLB | — |
| — | Shed | |

Works No 2 diagram **next week**

## Main line diesel locomotive diagrams
## Eastern Region: King's Cross

### Locomotive Diagram KX2

| Arrive | | Depart |
|---|---|---|
| **Monday** | | |
| — | Shed | 7 30am |
| — | King's Cross | 8 0am**(A)** |
| 12 16pm | Newcastle | 12 19pm |
| 2 19pm | Edinburgh | — |
| — | Haymarket Shed (Fuel) | |
| — | Haymarket Shed | 3 20pm |
| — | Edinburgh | 4 0pm**(A)** |
| 5 55pm | Newcastle | 5 58pm |
| 10 0pm | King's Cross | — |
| — | Shed (Fuel and Insp) | |
| | **Stand pilot 10 30pm to 4 30pm** | |
| **Tuesday** | | |
| — | Shed | 4 55pm |
| — | King's Cross | 5 25pm |
| 8 40pm | Leeds Central | 10 0pm |
| **Wednesday** | | |
| 3 25am | King's Cross | — |
| — | Shed | |
| — | Finsbury Park MD (Maintenance) | |
| — | Finsbury Park MD | 3 0pm |
| — | King's Cross | 4 0pm |
| 8 1pm | Newcastle | 8 4pm |
| 10 0pm | Edinburgh | — |
| — | Haymarket Shed (Fuel and Insp) | |
| — | Haymarket Shed | 11 10pm |
| — | Edinburgh | 11 50pm |
| **Thursday** | | |
| 2 12am | Newcastle | 2 20am |
| 7 33am | King's Cross | — |
| — | Shed (Fuel and Insp) | |
| — | Shed | 9 30am |
| — | King's Cross | 10 0am |
| 2 1pm | Newcastle | 2 4pm |
| 4 0pm | Edinburgh | — |
| — | Haymarket Shed (Fuel and Insp) | |
| — | Haymarket Shed | 9 21pm |
| — | Edinburgh | 10 1pm |
| **Friday** | | |
| 12 9am | Newcastle | 12 11am |
| 5 28am | Holloway CLB | — |
| — | Shed (Fuel) | |
| — | Shed | 7 30am |
| — | King's Cross | 8 0am |

| Arrive | | Depart |
|---|---|---|
| 12 16pm | Newcastle | 12 19pm |
| 2 19pm | Edinburgh | — |
| — | Haymarket Shed (Fuel) | |
| — | Haymarket Shed | 3 20pm |
| — | Edinburgh | 4 0pm**(B)** |
| 5 55pm | Newcastle | 5 58pm |
| 10 0am | King's Cross | — |
| — | Shed (Fuel and Insp) | |
| | **Stand Pilot 10 30pm to 4 30pm** | |
| **Saturday** | | |
| — | Shed | 4 55pm |
| — | King's Cross | 5 25pm |
| 8 40pm | Leeds Central | 10 0pm |
| **Sunday** | | |
| 3 25pm | King's Cross | — |
| — | Shed (Fuel) | |
| — | Shed | 11 30am |
| — | King's Cross | 12 0 noon |
| 5 51pm | Newcastle | 5 57pm |
| 8 20pm | Edinburgh | — |
| — | Haymarket Shed (Fuel and Insp) | |
| — | Haymarket Shed | 10 10pm |
| — | Edinburgh | 10 50pm |
| **Monday** | | |
| 1 14am | Newcastle | 1 22am |
| 2 50am | York | 2 57am |
| 5 0am | Grantham | |
| 7 21am | King's Cross | — |
| — | Shed | |

Work No 3 diagram **next week**

## Main line diesel locomotive diagrams
## Eastern Region: King's Cross

### Locomotive Diagram KX3

| Arrive | | Depart |
|---|---|---|
| **Monday** | | |
| — | Shed | 9 30am |
| — | King's Cross | 10 0am |
| 2 1pm | Newcastle | 2 4pm |
| 4 0pm | Edinburgh | — |
| — | Haymarket Shed (Fuel and Insp) | |
| — | Haymarket Shed | 9 21pm |
| — | Edinburgh | 10 1pm |
| **Tuesday** | | |
| 12 9am | Newcastle | 12 11am |
| 5 28am | Holloway CLB | — |
| — | Shed (Fuel and Insp) | |
| — | Shed | 7 30am |
| 12 16pm | Newcastle | 12 19pm |
| 2 19pm | Edinburgh | — |
| — | Haymarket Shed (Fuel) | |
| — | Haymarket Shed | 3 20pm |
| — | Edinburgh | 4 0pm |
| 5 55pm | Newcastle | 5 58pm |
| 10 0pm | King's Cross | — |
| — | Shed (Fuel and Insp) | |
| | **Stand Pilot 10 30pm to 4 30pm** | |
| **Wednesday** | | |
| — | Shed | 4 55pm |
| — | King's Cross | 5 25pm |
| 8 40pm | Leeds Central | 10 0pm |
| **Thursday** | | |
| 3 25am | King's Cross | — |
| — | Finsbury Park MD (Maintenance) | |
| — | Shed | 3 30pm |
| — | King's Cross | 4 0pm |
| 8 1pm | Newcastle | 8 4pm |
| 10 0pm | Edinburgh | — |
| — | Haymarket Shed (Fuel and Insp) | |
| — | Haymarket Shed | 11 10pm |
| — | Edinburgh | 11 50pm |
| **Friday** | | |
| 2 12am | Newcastle | 2 20am |
| 7 35am | King's Cross | — |

| *Arrive* | | *Depart* |
|---|---|---|
| — | Shed | |
| | (Fuel) | |
| | Shed | 9 30am |
| — | King's Cross | 10 0am |
| 2 1pm | Newcastle | 2 4pm |
| 4 0pm | Edinburgh | — |
| — | Haymarket Shed | |
| | (Fuel and Insp) | |
| | Haymarket Shed | 7 25pm |
| — | Edinburgh | 8 5pm |
| 11 7pm | Newcastle | 11 25pm |
| **Saturday** | | |
| 5 55am | King's Cross | — |
| — | Shed | |
| | (Fuel) | |
| | Shed | 12 15pm |
| — | King's Cross | 12 45pm |
| 4 30pm | Leeds Central | 5 29pm |
| 9 33pm | King's Cross | — |
| — | Shed | |
| | (Fuel and Insp) | |
| | Shed | 11 25pm |
| — | King's Cross | 11 55pm |
| **Sunday** | | |
| — | Doncaster | 3 40am |
| 6 39am | Newcastle | 6 40am |
| 6 47am | Heaton Shed | |
| | Heaton Shed | 12 43pm |
| — | HCS | 12 53pm |
| 1 3pm | Newcastle | 1 22pm |
| 4 35pm | Doncaster | 4 39pm |
| 5 54pm | Peterborough | — |
| 7 49pm | King's Cross | — |
| — | Shed | |
| | (Fuel) | |

Work No 4 diagram **next week.**

**Main line diesel locomotive diagrams**
**Eastern Region: King's Cross**

**Locomotive Diagram KX4**

| | | |
|---|---|---|
| **Sunday** | | |
| | Shed | 11 15pm |
| — | King's Cross | 11 45pm |
| **Monday** | | |
| — | Grantham | 1 56am |
| 4 10am | York | 4 22am |
| 6 14am | Newcastle | 6 15am |
| 6 25am | Gateshead Shed | |
| | (Fuel) | |
| | Gateshead Shed | 7 35am |
| — | Newcastle | 7 50am |
| 12 5pm | King's Cross | — |
| — | Shed | |
| | (Fuel) | |
| | Shed | 3 30pm |
| — | King's Cross | 4 0pm |
| 8 1pm | Newcastle | 8 4pm |
| 10 pm | Edinburgh | — |
| — | Haymarket Shed | |
| | (Fuel and Insp) | |
| | Haymarket Shed | 11 10pm |
| — | Edinburgh | 11 50pm |
| **Tuesday** | | |
| 2 12am | Newcastle | 2 20am |
| 7 35am | King's Cross | — |
| — | Shed | |
| | (Fuel) | |
| | Shed | 9 30am |
| — | King's Cross | 10 0am |
| 2 1pm | Newcastle | 2 4pm |
| 4 0pm | Edinburgh | — |
| — | Haymarket Shed | |
| | (Fuel and Insp) | |
| | Haymarket Shed | 9 21pm |
| — | Edinburgh | 10 1pm |
| **Wednesday** | | |
| 12 9am | Newcastle | 21 11am |
| 5 28am | Holloway CLB | — |
| — | Shed | |
| | (Fuel) | |
| | Shed | 7 30am |
| — | King's Cross | 8 0am |
| 12 16pm | Newcastle | 12 19pm |

| *Arrive* | | *Depart* |
|---|---|---|
| 2 19 | Edinburgh | — |
| — | Haymarket Shed | |
| | (Fuel) | |
| | Haymarket Shed | 3 20pm |
| — | Edinburgh | 4 0pm |
| 5 55pm | Newcastle | 5 58pm |
| 10 0pm | King's Cross | — |
| — | Shed | |
| | (Fuel and Insp) | |
| | **Pilot 10 30pm to 4 30pm** | |
| **Thursday** | | |
| | Shed | 4 55pm |
| — | King's Cross | 5 25pm |
| 8 40pm | Leeds Central | 10 0pm |
| **Friday** | | |
| 3 25am | King's Cross | — |
| — | Finsbury Park MD | |
| | (Maintenance) | |
| | Finsbury Park MD | — |
| — | King's Cross | 4 0pm |
| 8 1pm | Newcastle | 8 4pm |
| 10 4pm | Edinburgh | — |
| — | Haymarket Shed | |
| | (Fuel and Insp) | |
| | Haymarket Shed | 11 10pm |
| — | Edinburgh | 11 50pm |
| **Saturday** | | |
| 2 12am | Newcastle | 2 20am |
| 7 33am | King's Cross | — |
| — | Shed | |
| | (Fuel) | |
| | Shed | 10 30am |
| — | King's Cross | 11 0am |
| 4 15pm | Newcastle | 4 23pm |
| 6 32pm | Edinburgh | — |
| — | Haymarket Shed | |
| | (Fuel and Insp) | |
| | Haymarket Shed | 10 25pm |
| — | Edinburgh | 11 5pm |
| **Sunday** | | |
| 1 31am | Newcastle | 1 38am |
| 6 54am | King's Cross | |
| — | Shed | |
| | (Fuel) | |
| | Shed | 1 0pm |
| — | King's Cross | 1 30pm |
| 4 46pm | Doncaster | 6 37pm |
| 9 37pm | King's Cross | — |
| — | Shed | |
| | (Fuel and Insp) | |

Work No 5 diagram **next week**

**Main line diesel locomotive diagrams**
**Eastern Region: King's Cross**

**Locomotive Diagram KX5**

| | | |
|---|---|---|
| **Monday** | | |
| | Shed | 9 0am |
| — | King's Cross | 9 30am |
| 3 30pm | Edinburgh | — |
| — | Haymarket Shed | |
| | (Fuel and Insp) | |
| | Haymarket Shed | 7 25pm |
| — | Edinburgh | 8 0pm |
| 11 7pm | Newcastle | 11 25pm |
| **Tuesday** | | |
| 5 53am | King's Cross | — |
| — | Shed | |
| | (Fuel) | |
| | Shed | 9 0am |
| — | King's Cross | 9 30am |
| 3 30pm | Edinburgh | — |
| — | Haymarket Shed | |
| | (Fuel and Insp) | |
| | Haymarket Shed | 7 25pm |
| — | Edinburgh | 8 5pm |
| 11 7pm | Newcastle | 11 25pm |
| **Wednesday** | | |
| 5 53am | King's Cross | — |
| — | Shed | |
| | (Fuel) | |
| | Shed | 9 0am |
| — | King's Cross | 9 30am |
| 3 30pm | Edinburgh | — |

| Arrive | | Depart | |
|---|---|---|---|
| — | Haymarket Shed ... ... ... ... ... | | |
| | (Fuel and Insp) | | |
| | Haymarket Shed ... ... ... ... | 7 25pm | |
| — | Edinburgh ... ... ... ... | 8 5pm | SO |
| 11 7pm | Newcastle ... ... ... ... | 11 25pm | |
| **Thursday** | | | |
| 5 53am | King's Cross ... ... ... ... | — | |
| — | Shed ... ... ... ... | | |
| | (Fuel) | | |
| | Shed ... ... ... ... | 9 0am | |
| — | King's Cross ... ... ... | 9 30am | |
| 3 30pm | Edinburgh ... ... ... | — | |
| — | Haymarket Shed ... ... ... | | |
| | (Fuel and Insp) | | |
| | Haymarket Shed ... ... ... | 7 25pm | |
| — | Edinburgh ... ... ... ... | 8 5pm | |
| 11 7pm | Newcastle ... ... ... ... | 11 25pm | |
| **Friday** | | | |
| 5 53am | King's Cross ... ... ... ... | — | |
| — | Shed ... ... ... ... | | |
| | (Fuel) | | |
| | Shed ... ... ... ... | 9 0am | |
| — | King's Cross ... ... ... | 9 30am | |
| 3 30pm | Edinburgh ... ... ... | — | |
| — | Haymarket Shed ... ... ... | | |
| | (Fuel and Insp) | | |
| | Haymarket Shed ... ... ... | 9 21pm | |
| — | Edinburgh ... ... ... ... | 10 1pm | |
| **Saturday** | | | |
| 12 9am | Newcastle ... ... ... ... | 12 11am | |
| 5 28am | Holloway CLB ... ... ... | — | |
| — | Shed ... ... ... ... | | |
| | (Fuel) | | |
| | Shed ... ... ... ... | 7 15am | |
| — | King's Cross ... ... ... | 7 45am | |
| 11 50am | Leeds Central ... ... ... | 2 10pm | |
| 6 26pm | King's Cross ... ... ... | — | |
| — | Finsbury Park MD ... ... ... | | |
| | (Maintenance) | | |
| **Sunday** | | | |
| — | Finsbury Park MD ... ... ... | — | |
| — | King's Cross ... ... ... ... | | |

**Stand Pilot 12 0 noon Sun to 9 30pm Mon**
Work No 6 diagram **next week**

### Main line diesel locomotive diagrams
### Eastern Region: King's Cross

#### Locomotive Diagram KX6

| Arrive | | Depart | |
|---|---|---|---|
| — | Shed ... ... ... ... | 9 45pm | SX |
| — | King's Cross ... ... ... ... | 10 15pm | |
| 2 48am | Newcastle ... ... ... ... | 2 55am | |
| 5 12am | Edinburgh ... ... ... | — | |
| — | Haymarket Shed ... ... ... | | |
| | (Fuel and Insp) | | MX |
| | Haymarket Shed ... ... ... | 9 20am | |
| — | Edinburgh ... ... ... | 10 0am | |
| 11 55am | Newcastle ... ... ... ... | 11 58am | |
| 4 0pm | King's Cross ... ... ... | — | |
| — | Shed ... ... ... | | |

**Stand Pilot 5 0pm to 9 0pm MSX**

| Arrive | | Depart | |
|---|---|---|---|
| 4 0pm | King's Cross ... ... ... | — | |
| — | Finsbury Park MD ... ... ... | | SO |
| | (Maintenance) | | |
| | Finsbury Park MD ... ... ... | 8 40am | |
| | King's Cross ... ... ... | 9 40am | |
| 1 18pm | Leeds Central ... ... ... | 4 20pm | SuO |
| 8 0pm | King's Cross ... ... ... | — | |
| — | Shed ... ... ... | | |
| | (Fuel and Insp) | | |

Works No 1 diagram next week

#### Locomotive Diagram KX7

| | Arrive | | Depart | |
|---|---|---|---|---|
| SX | — | Finsbury Park MD ... ... ... | 10 0am | MO |
| | — | Shed ... ... ... | 10 30am | MSX |
| | — | King's Cross ... ... ... | 11 0am | |
| | 4 6pm | Newcastle ... ... ... | 4 14pm | |
| | 6 32pm | Edinburgh ... ... ... | — | |
| | — | Haymarket Shed ... ... ... | | |
| | | (Fuel and Insp) | | |
| | | Haymarket Shed ... ... ... | 10 10pm | |
| | — | Edinburgh ... ... ... | 10 50pm | |
| | 1 14am | Newcastle ... ... ... | 1 22am | |

| Arrive | | Depart | |
|---|---|---|---|
| 7 21am | King's Cross ... ... ... ... | — | MX |
| — | Shed ... ... ... ... | | |
| | (Fuel and Insp) | | |
| | Shed ... ... ... ... | 2 0pm | |
| — | King's Cross ... ... ... | 2 30pm | |
| 4 24pm | Grantham ... ... ... | 4 30pm | |
| 6 10pm | York ... ... ... | 6 16pm | |
| 7 57pm | Newcastle ... ... ... | 8 6pm | |
| 8 16pm | HCS | | |
| — | Gateshead Shed ... ... ... | | |
| | (Fuel and Insp) | | |
| | Gateshead Shed ... ... ... | 3 0pm | |
| — | Newcastle ... ... ... | 3 15pm | SuO |
| 9 29pm | King's Cross ... ... ... | — | |
| — | Finsbury Park MD ... ... ... | | |
| | (Maintenance) | | |

Works No 8 diagram next week

#### Locomotive Diagram KX8

| Arrive | | Depart | |
|---|---|---|---|
| — | Finsbury Park MD ... ... ... | 12 1am | MO |
| — | Shed ... ... ... ... | 12 25am | MX |
| — | King's Cross ... ... ... | 12 55am | |
| 6 29am | Newcastle ... ... ... | 6 55am | |
| 9 46am | Edinburgh ... ... ... | — | |
| — | Haymarket Shed ... ... ... | | |
| | (Fuel) | | |
| | Haymarket Shed ... ... ... | 11 25am | |
| — | Edinburgh ... ... ... | 12 5pm(A) | |
| 2 15pm | Newcastle ... ... ... | 2 20pm | |
| 4 27pm | Leeds Central ... ... ... | 5 10pm | |
| 6 1pm | Doncaster ... ... ... | 6 22pm | SX |
| 9 40pm | King's Cross ... ... ... | — | |
| — | Shed ... ... ... | | |
| — | Leeds Central ... ... ... | 5 43pm | |
| 6 41pm | Doncaster ... ... ... | 7 28pm | SO |
| 10 26pm | King's Cross ... ... ... | — | |
| — | Finsbury Park MD ... ... ... | | |

Works No 7 diagram next week.
**(A) does not run 6 August**

### Main line diesel locomotive diagrams
### Scottish Region: Haymarket

#### Locomotive Diagram HT2A

**Stand Pilot 9 0am Mon to 9 0am Sat**
(Maintenance)

| Arrive | | Depart | |
|---|---|---|---|
| **Saturday** | | | |
| — | Shed ... ... ... ... | 9 34pm | |
| — | Haymarket Goods Loop ... ... | 9 54pm | |
| 10 12pm | Edinburgh ... ... ... ... | 10 30pm | |
| **Sunday** | | | |
| 1 1am | Newcastle ... ... ... | 1 9am | |
| 6 24am | King's Cross ... ... ... | — | |
| — | Shed ... ... ... | | |
| | (Fuel) | | |
| | Shed ... ... ... | 7 0pm | |
| — | King's Cross ... ... ... | 7 30pm | |
| **Monday** | | | |
| 12 44am | Newcastle ... ... ... | 12 54am | |
| 3 0am | Edinburgh ... ... ... | — | |
| — | Shed ... ... ... | | |
| | (Fuel and Insp) | | |

Works No 2 diagram next week

#### Locomotive Diagram HT2B

| Arrive | | Depart | |
|---|---|---|---|
| — | Shed ... ... ... ... | 9 5am | |
| — | Edinburgh ... ... ... ... | 9 45am | |
| 3 45pmR | King's Cross ... ... ... ... | — | SX |
| — | Shed ... ... ... ... | | |
| | (Fuel) | | |
| | Shed ... ... ... ... | 7 50pm | |
| — | King's Cross ... ... ... ... | 8 20pm | FSX |
| — | Doncaster ... ... ... ... | 11 40pm | |
| 2 5am† | Newcastle ... ... ... | 2 17am | |
| 4 40am | Edinburgh ... ... ... | — | MSX |
| — | Shed ... ... ... | | |
| | Shed ... ... ... | 7 0pm | FO |
| — | King's Cross ... ... ... | 7 30pm | |
| 12 44am | Newcastle ... ... ... | 12 54am | |
| 3 0am | Edinburgh ... ... ... | — | SO |
| — | Shed ... ... ... | | |
| | (Maintenance) | | |

| Arrive | | | Depart | |
|---|---|---|---|---|
| — | Shed | ... ... ... ... ... | 12 50pm | |
| | Edinburgh | ... ... ... ... ... | 1 30pm | |
| 3 35pm | Newcastle | ... ... ... ... ... | 4 0pm | SO |
| 6 31pm | Grantham | ... ... ... ... ... | 6 36pm | |
| 8 23pm | King's Cross | ... ... ... ... ... | — | |
| — | Shed | | | |
| | (Fuel) | | | |
| | **Stand Pilot 10 0pm Sat to 12 0 noon Sun** | | | |
| | Shed | ... ... ... ... ... | 1 30pm | |
| — | King's Cross | ... ... ... ... ... | 2 0pm | |
| 7 23pm | Newcastle | ... ... ... ... ... | 7 29pm | SuO |
| 9 39pm | Edinburgh | ... ... ... ... ... | — | |
| — | Shed | | | |
| | **Stand Pilot 10 30pm Sun to 9 0am Mon** | | | |
| | (Fuel and Insp) | | | |

Works No 3 diagram next week

### Main line diesel locomotive diagrams
### Scottish Region: Haymarket

#### Locomotive Diagram HT2C

| Arrive | | | Depart |
|---|---|---|---|
| **Monday** | | | |
| — | Shed | ... ... ... ... ... | 12 50pm |
| | Edinburgh | ... ... ... ... ... | 1 30pm |
| 3 35pm | Newcastle | ... ... ... ... ... | 3 41pm |
| 6 31pm | Grantham | ... ... ... ... ... | 6 36pm |
| 8 23pm | King's Cross | ... ... ... ... ... | — |
| — | Shed (Fuel) | ... ... ... ... ... | |
| | Shed | ... ... ... ... ... | 10 15pm |
| | King's Cross | ... ... ... ... ... | 10 45pm |
| **Tuesday** | | | |
| 2 8am | Doncaster | ... ... ... ... ... | 2 22am |
| 3 22am | Leeds Central | ... ... ... ... ... | 7 30am |
| 10 30am | King's Cross | ... ... ... ... ... | — |
| — | Shed | | |
| | (Fuel and Insp) | | |
| | Shed | ... ... ... ... ... | 1 30pm |
| — | King's Cross | ... ... ... ... ... | 2 0pm |
| 5 12pm | York | ... ... ... ... ... | 5 16pm |
| 6 41pm | Newcastle | ... ... ... ... ... | 6 46pm |
| 9 0pm | Edinburgh | ... ... ... ... ... | — |
| — | Shed (Fuel) | ... ... ... ... ... | |
| | Shed | ... ... ... ... ... | 10 25pm |
| — | Edinburgh | ... ... ... ... ... | 11 5pm |
| **Wednesday** | | | |
| 1 30am | Newcastle | ... ... ... ... ... | 1 38am |
| 6 48am | King's Cross | ... ... ... ... ... | — |
| — | Shed | | |
| | (Fuel and Insp) | | |
| | Shed | ... ... ... ... ... | 9 10am |
| — | King's Cross | ... ... ... ... ... | 9 40am |
| 12 9pm | Doncaster | ... ... ... ... ... | 12 58pm |
| 2 0pm | Leeds Central | ... ... ... ... ... | 5 29pm |
| 8 42pm | King's Cross | ... ... ... ... ... | — |
| — | Shed (Fuel) | ... ... ... ... ... | |
| | Shed | ... ... ... ... ... | 10 0pm |
| — | King's Cross | ... ... ... ... ... | 10 30pm |
| **Thursday** | | | |
| 3 49am† | Newcastle | ... ... ... ... ... | 3 59am |
| 4 9am | Gateshead Shed | ... ... ... ... ... | |
| | (Fuel and Insp) | | |
| | Gateshead Shed | ... ... ... ... ... | 9 25am |
| — | Newcastle | ... ... ... ... ... | 9 40am |
| 2 28pm | King's Cross | ... ... ... ... ... | — |
| — | Shed (Fuel) | ... ... ... ... ... | |
| | Shed | ... ... ... ... ... | 7 0pm |
| | King's Cross | ... ... ... ... ... | 7 30pm |
| **Friday** | | | |
| 12 44am | Newcastle | ... ... ... ... ... | 12 54am |
| 3 0am | Edinburgh | ... ... ... ... ... | — |
| — | Shed (Maintenance) | ... ... ... ... ... | |
| | Shed | ... ... ... ... ... | 12 50pm |
| | Edinburgh | ... ... ... ... ... | 1 30pm |
| 3 35pm | Newcastle | ... ... ... ... ... | 3 41pm |
| 8 23pm | King's Cross | ... ... ... ... ... | — |
| — | Shed (Fuel) | ... ... ... ... ... | |
| | Shed | ... ... ... ... ... | 10 0pm |
| — | King's Cross | ... ... ... ... ... | 10 30pm |
| **Saturday** | | | |
| 3 49am† | Newcastle | ... ... ... ... ... | 3 59am |
| 4 9am | Gateshead Shed | ... ... ... ... ... | |
| | (Fuel and Insp) | | |
| | Gateshead Shed | ... ... ... ... ... | 7 45am |
| — | Newcastle | ... ... ... ... ... | 8 0am |

| Arrive | | | Depart |
|---|---|---|---|
| 11 0am | Grantham | ... ... ... ... ... | — |
| 1 5pm | King's Cross | ... ... ... ... ... | — |
| — | Shed (Fuel) | | |
| — | Shed | ... ... ... ... ... | 7 50pm |
| | King's Cross | ... ... ... ... ... | 8 20pm |
| | Doncaster | ... ... ... ... ... | 11 40pm |
| **Sunday** | | | |
| 12 16am | York | ... ... ... ... ... | 12 26am |
| 2 5am | Newcastle | ... ... ... ... ... | 2 17am |
| 4 33am | Edinburgh | ... ... ... ... ... | — |
| — | Shed | | |
| | (Fuel and Insp) | | |
| | Shed | ... ... ... ... ... | 11 20am |
| — | Edinburgh | ... ... ... ... ... | 12 0 noon |
| 2 30pm | Newcastle | ... ... ... ... ... | 2 38pm |
| 5 15pm | Doncaster | ... ... ... ... ... | — |
| 8 45pm | King's Cross | ... ... ... ... ... | — |
| — | Shed (Fuel) | ... ... ... ... ... | |
| | Shed | ... ... ... ... ... | 11 40pm |
| **Monday** | | | |
| — | King's Cross | ... ... ... ... ... | 12 10am |
| 3 52am | Doncaster | ... ... ... ... ... | 3 27am |
| 6 44am | Leeds Central | ... ... ... ... ... | 7 30am |
| 10 30am | King's Cross | ... ... ... ... ... | — |
| — | Shed | | |
| | (Fuel and Insp) | | |
| | Shed | ... ... ... ... ... | 1 30pm |
| — | King's Cross | ... ... ... ... ... | 2 0pm |
| 5 12pm | York | ... ... ... ... ... | 5 16pm |
| 6 41pm | Newcastle | ... ... ... ... ... | 6 46pm |
| 9 0pm | Edinburgh | ... ... ... ... ... | — |
| — | Shed (Fuel) | ... ... ... ... ... | |

Works No 4 diagram next week.

### Main line diesel locomotive diagrams
### Scottish Region: Haymarket

#### Locomotive Diagram HT2D

| Arrive | | | Depart |
|---|---|---|---|
| **Monday** | | | |
| | Shed | ... ... ... ... ... | 10 35pm |
| — | Edinburgh | ... ... ... ... ... | 11 5pm |
| **Tuesday** | | | |
| 1 31am | Newcastle | ... ... ... ... ... | 1 38am |
| 6 48am | King's Cross | ... ... ... ... ... | — |
| — | Shed | | |
| | (Fuel and Insp) | | |
| | Shed | ... ... ... ... ... | 9 10am |
| — | King's Cross | ... ... ... ... ... | 9 40am |
| 12 9pm | Doncaster | ... ... ... ... ... | 12 58pm |
| 2 0pm | Leeds Central | ... ... ... ... ... | 5 29pm |
| 8 42pm | King's Cross | ... ... ... ... ... | — |
| — | Shed | | |
| | (Fuel) | | |
| | Shed | ... ... ... ... ... | 10 0pm |
| — | King's Cross | ... ... ... ... ... | 10 30pm |
| **Wednesday** | | | |
| 3 49am† | Newcastle | ... ... ... ... ... | 3 59am |
| 4 9am | Gateshead Shed | ... ... ... ... ... | |
| | (Fuel and Insp) | | |
| | Gateshead Shed | ... ... ... ... ... | 9 25am |
| — | Newcastle | ... ... ... ... ... | 9 40am |
| 2 28pm | King's Cross | ... ... ... ... ... | — |
| — | Shed | | |
| | (Fuel) | | |
| | Shed | ... ... ... ... ... | 7 0pm |
| — | King's Cross | ... ... ... ... ... | 7 30pm |
| **Thursday** | | | |
| 12 44am | Newcastle | ... ... ... ... ... | 12 54am |
| 3 0am | Edinburgh | ... ... ... ... ... | — |
| — | Shed | | |
| | (Maintenance) | | |
| | Shed | ... ... ... ... ... | 1 0pm |
| | Edinburgh | ... ... ... ... ... | 1 30pm |
| 3 35pm | Newcastle | ... ... ... ... ... | 3 41pm |
| 6 31pm | Grantham | ... ... ... ... ... | 6 36pm |
| 8 23pm | King's Cross | ... ... ... ... ... | — |
| — | Shed | | |
| | (Fuel) | | |
| | Shed | ... ... ... ... ... | 10 15pm |
| — | King's Cross | ... ... ... ... ... | 10 45pm |
| **Friday** | | | |
| 2 8am | Doncaster | ... ... ... ... ... | 2 22am |
| 3 22am | Leeds | ... ... ... ... ... | 7 30am |

| Arrive | | | | | | | Depart |
|---|---|---|---|---|---|---|---|
| 10 30am | King's Cross | ... | ... | ... | ... | ... | — |
| — | Shed | | | | | | |
| | (Fuel and Insp) | | | | | | |
| | Shed | | | ... | ... | ... | 1 30pm |
| — | King's Cross | ... | ... | ... | ... | ... | 2 0pm |
| 5 12pm | York | ... | ... | ... | ... | ... | 5 16pm |
| 6 41pm | Newcastle | ... | ... | ... | ... | | 6 46pm |
| 9 0pm | Edinburgh | ... | ... | ... | ... | | — |
| — | Shed | | | | | | |
| | (Fuel) | | | | | | |
| | Shed | | | | ... | ... | 10 25pm |
| — | Edinburgh | | | ... | ... | ... | 11 5pm |
| **Saturday** | | | | | | | |
| 1 31am | Newcastle | | | | | | 1 38am |
| 6 48am | King's Cross | | | | | | — |
| | Shed | ... | | | | | |
| | (Fuel and Insp) | | | | | | |
| | Shed | | | | | | 11 30am |
| — | King's Cross | ... | ... | ... | ... | ... | 12 0 noon |
| 3 22pm | Leeds Central | | | | | | 4 36pm |
| 7 49pm | King's Cross | ... | ... | ... | ... | ... | — |
| | Shed | ... | ... | ... | ... | ... | |
| | (Fuel) | | | | | | |
| | Shed | | | | | | 9 45pm |
| — | King's Cross | | | | | | 10 15pm |
| **Sunday** | | | | | | | |
| 2 48am | Newcastle | ... | ... | ... | ... | | 2 55am |
| 5 0am | Edinburgh | ... | ... | ... | ... | | — |
| — | Shed | ... | ... | ... | | | |
| | (Fuel and Insp) | | | | | | |

**Stand Pilot 9 0am to 9 0pm Sun**

Works No 5 diagram next week

### Main line diesel locomotive diagrams
### Scottish Region: Haymarket

### Locomotive Diagram HT2E

| | | | | | | | |
|---|---|---|---|---|---|---|---|
| **Sunday** | | | | | | | |
| | Shed | ... | ... | ... | ... | | 10 25pm |
| — | Edinburgh | ... | ... | ... | ... | | 11 5pm |
| **Monday** | | | | | | | |
| 1 31am | Newcastle | | | | ... | | 1 38am |
| 6 48am | King's Cross | ... | ... | ... | | | — |
| | Shed | ... | | | | | |
| | (Fuel and Insp) | | | | | | |
| | Shed | | | | | | 9 10am |
| — | King's Cross | | | | | | 9 40am |
| 12 9pm | Doncaster | ... | ... | ... | ... | | 12 58pm |
| 2 0pm | Leeds Central | | | | | | 5 29pm |
| 8 42pm | King's Cross | ... | ... | ... | | | — |
| — | Shed (Fuel) | | | | | | |
| | Shed | ... | ... | ... | ... | | 10 0pm |
| — | King's Cross | ... | ... | ... | | | 10 30pm |
| **Tuesday** | | | | | | | |
| 3 49am† | Newcastle | ... | ... | ... | | | 3 59am |
| 4 9am | Gateshead Shed | ... | | | | | |
| | (Fuel and Insp) | | | | | | |
| | Gateshead Shed | ... | | | | | 9 25am |
| — | Newcastle | | | | | | 9 40am |
| 2 28pm | King's Cross | ... | ... | ... | | | — |
| — | Shed (Fuel) | | | | | | |
| | Shed | ... | ... | ... | ... | | 7 0pm |
| — | King's Cross | ... | ... | ... | | | 7 30pm |
| **Wednesday** | | | | | | | |
| 12 44am | Newcastle | ... | ... | ... | | | 12 54am |
| 3 0am | Edinburgh | ... | ... | ... | ... | | |
| | Shed | | | | | | |
| | (Maintenance) | | | | | | |
| | Shed | ... | ... | ... | | | 12 50pm |
| — | Edinburgh | ... | ... | ... | | | 1 30pm |
| 3 35pm | Newcastle | ... | ... | ... | | | 3 41pm |
| 6 30pm | Grantham | ... | ... | ... | ... | | — |
| 8 23pm | King's Cross | ... | ... | ... | | | — |
| — | Shed (Fuel) | ... | ... | ... | | | |
| | Shed | ... | ... | ... | ... | | 10 15pm |
| — | King's Cross | ... | ... | ... | | | 10 45pm |
| **Thursday** | | | | | | | |
| 2 8am | Doncaster | ... | ... | ... | ... | | 2 22am |
| 3 22am | Leeds Central | ... | ... | ... | | | 7 30am |
| 10 30am | King's Cross | ... | ... | ... | | | — |
| | Shed | ... | ... | ... | ... | | |
| | (Fuel and Insp) | | | | | | |
| | Shed | | | | | | 1 30pm |

| Arrive | | | | | | | Depart |
|---|---|---|---|---|---|---|---|
| — | King's Cross | | | | | | 2 0pm |
| 5 12pm | York | ... | ... | ... | ... | | 5 16pm |
| 6 41pm | Newcastle | ... | ... | ... | ... | | 6 46pm |
| 9 0pm | Edinburgh | ... | ... | ... | ... | | — |
| — | Shed (Fuel) | ... | ... | ... | | | |
| | Shed | ... | ... | ... | ... | | 10 25pm |
| — | Edinburgh | ... | ... | ... | | | 11 5pm |
| **Friday** | | | | | | | |
| 1 31am | Newcastle | ... | ... | ... | | | 1 38am |
| 6 48am | King's Cross | ... | ... | ... | | | — |
| — | Shed | ... | ... | ... | | | |
| | (Fuel and Insp) | | | | | | |
| | Shed | ... | ... | ... | | | 9 10am |
| — | King's Cross | ... | ... | ... | | | 9 40am |
| 12 9pm | Doncaster | ... | ... | ... | ... | | 12 58pm |
| 2 0pm | Leeds Central | ... | ... | ... | | | 5 29pm |
| 8 42pm | King's Cross | ... | ... | ... | | | — |
| — | Shed (Fuel) | ... | ... | ... | | | |
| | Shed | ... | ... | ... | ... | | 10 15pm |
| — | King's Cross | ... | ... | ... | | | 10 45pm |
| **Saturday** | | | | | | | |
| 2 8am | Doncaster | ... | ... | ... | ... | | 2 22am |
| 3 22pm | Leeds Central | ... | ... | ... | | | 7 30am |
| 10 48am | King's Cross | ... | ... | ... | | | — |
| — | Shed | ... | ... | ... | | | |
| | (Fuel and Insp) | | | | | | |
| | Shed | ... | ... | ... | ... | | 1 0pm |
| — | King's Cross | ... | ... | ... | | | 1 30pm |
| — | Grantham | ... | ... | ... | | | 3 25pm |
| 4 58pm | York | ... | ... | ... | ... | | 5 3pm |
| 6 30pm | Newcastle | ... | ... | ... | | | 6 37pm |
| 8 54pm | Edinburgh | ... | ... | ... | | | |
| | Shed (Fuel) | ... | ... | ... | | | |
| | Shed | ... | ... | ... | ... | | 11 10pm |
| — | Edinburgh | ... | ... | ... | | | 11 50pm |
| **Sunday** | | | | | | | |
| 2 22am | Newcastle | ... | ... | ... | | | 2 30am |
| 7 46am | King's Cross | ... | ... | ... | | | — |
| — | Shed | ... | ... | ... | | | |
| | (Fuel and Insp) | | | | | | |
| | Shed | ... | ... | ... | ... | | 7 50pm |
| | King's Cross | ... | ... | ... | | | 8 20pm |
| — | Grantham | ... | ... | ... | | | 10 22pm |
| **Monday** | | | | | | | |
| 12 16am | York | ... | ... | ... | ... | | 12 26am |
| 2 5am | Newcastle | ... | ... | ... | | | 2 17am |
| 4 40am | Edinburgh | ... | ... | ... | | | — |
| — | Shed | ... | ... | ... | ... | | |
| | (Fuel and Insp) | | | | | | |

Work No 6 diagram next week

### Main line diesel locomotive diagrams
### Scottish Region: Haymarket

### Locomotive Diagram HT2F

| | | | | | | | |
|---|---|---|---|---|---|---|---|
| **Monday** | | | | | | | |
| | Shed | ... | ... | ... | ... | | 9 20am |
| — | Edinburgh | ... | ... | ... | ... | | 10 0am |
| 11 55am | Newcastle | ... | ... | ... | ... | | 11 58am |
| 4 0pm | King's Cross | ... | ... | ... | | | — |
| — | Shed | ... | ... | ... | ... | | |
| | (Fuel) | | | | | | |
| | Shed | ... | ... | ... | ... | | 7 0pm |
| — | King's Cross | ... | ... | ... | | | 7 30pm |
| **Tuesday** | | | | | | | |
| 12 44am | Newcastle | ... | ... | ... | | | 12 54am |
| 3 0am | Edinburgh | ... | ... | ... | | | |
| | Shed | ... | ... | ... | | | |
| | (Maintenance) | | | | | | |
| | Shed | ... | ... | ... | | | 12 50pm |
| — | Edinburgh | ... | ... | ... | | | 1 30pm |
| 3 35pm | Newcastle | ... | ... | ... | | | 3 41pm |
| 6 31pm | Grantham | ... | ... | ... | | | — |
| 8 23pm | King's Cross | ... | ... | ... | | | — |
| — | Shed | ... | ... | ... | | | |
| | (Fuel) | | | | | | |
| | Shed | ... | ... | ... | ... | | 10 15pm |
| — | King's Cross | ... | ... | ... | | | 10 45pm |
| **Wednesday** | | | | | | | |
| 2 8am | Doncaster | ... | ... | ... | ... | | 2 22am |
| 3 22am | Leeds | ... | ... | ... | | | 7 30am |

| Arrive | Location | Depart | Flag |
|---|---|---|---|
| 10 30am | King's Cross | — | |
| — | Shed (Fuel and Insp) | | |
| — | Shed | 1 30pm | |
| — | King's Cross | 2 0pm | |
| 5 12pm | York | 5 16pm | |
| 6 41pm | Newcastle | 6 46pm | |
| 9 0pm | Edinburgh | — | |
| — | Shed (Fuel) | | |
| — | Shed | 10 25pm | |
| — | Edinburgh | 11 5pm | |

**Thursday**

| Arrive | Location | Depart | Flag |
|---|---|---|---|
| 1 31am | Newcastle | 1 38am | |
| 6 48am | King's Cross | — | |
| — | Shed (Fuel and Insp) | | |
| — | Shed | 9 10am | |
| — | King's Cross | 9 40am | |
| 12 9pm | Doncaster | 12 58pm | |
| 2 0pm | Leeds Central | 5 29pm | |
| 8 42pm | King's Cross | — | |
| — | Shed (Fuel) | | |
| — | Shed | 10 0pm | |
| — | King's Cross | 10 30pm | |

**Friday**

| Arrive | Location | Depart | Flag |
|---|---|---|---|
| 3 49am† | Newcastle | 3 59am | |
| 4 9am | Gateshead Shed (Fuel and Insp) | | |
| — | Gateshead Shed | 9 25am | |
| — | Newcastle | 9 40am | |
| 2 28pm | King's Cross | — | |
| — | Shed (Fuel and Insp) | | |
| — | Shed | 7 50pm | |
| — | King's Cross | 8 20pm | |

**Saturday**

| Arrive | Location | Depart | Flag |
|---|---|---|---|
| 12 16am | York | 12 26am | |
| 2 5am | Newcastle | 2 17am | |
| 4 33am | Edinburgh | — | |
| — | Shed | | |

Stand Pilot 9 0am to 11 30pm SO
(Maintenance)

**Sunday**

| Arrive | Location | Depart | Flag |
|---|---|---|---|
| — | Shed | 9 30am | |
| — | Edinburgh | 10 10am | |
| 12 24pm | Newcastle | 12 30pm | |
| 5 49pm | King's Cross | — | |
| — | Shed (Fuel) | | |
| — | Shed | 9 45pm | |
| — | King's Cross | 10 15pm | |

**Monday**

| Arrive | Location | Depart | Flag |
|---|---|---|---|
| 2 48am | Newcastle | 2 55am | |
| 5 0am | Edinburgh | — | |
| — | Shed | | |

Works No 2A diagram next week

### Main line diesel locomotive diagrams
### Scottish Region: Haymarket

### Locomotive Diagram HT3A

| Arrive | Location | Depart | Flag |
|---|---|---|---|
| — | Shed | 10 20am | |
| —P | Edinburgh | 11 0am | |
| 1 22am | Newcastle | 1 30pm | |
| 5 12am | Peterborough | — | SX |
| 6 42am | King's Cross | — | |
| — | Shed (Fuel and Insp) | | |
| — | Shed | 11 5pm | |
| — | King's Cross | 11 35pm | |
| 4 55am | Newcastle | 5 3am | |
| 7 27am | Edinburgh | — | MX |
| — | Shed (Maintenance) SO | | |

Works No 3A diagram next week

### Locomotive Diagram HT3B

| Arrive | Location | Depart | Flag |
|---|---|---|---|
| — | (Fuel and Insp) | | |
| — | Shed | 9 34pm | |
| — | Haymarket Goods Loop | 9 54pm | SX |
| 10 12pm | Newcastle | 10 30pm | |

| Arrive | Location | Depart | Flag |
|---|---|---|---|
| 1 1am | Newcastle | 1 9am | |
| 6 24am | King's Cross | — | MX |
| — | Shed (Fuel) | | |
| — | Shed | 9 50am | |
| — | King's Cross | 10 20am | |
| 2 31pm | Leeds Cen | 3 39pm | |
| 5 47pm | Newcastle | 5 53pm | MSX |
| 7 59pm | Edinburgh | — | |
| — | Haymarket Shed | | |
| 2 31pm | Leeds Cen | 3 30pm | |
| 5 35pm | Newcastle | 5 41pm | SO |
| 7 49pm | Edinburgh | — | |
| — | Haymarket Shed (Maintenance) | | |
| — | Shed | 11 10pm | SuO |
| — | Edinburgh | 11 50pm | |
| 2 12am | Newcastle | 2 20am | |
| 7 33am | King's Cross | — | |
| — | Shed (Fuel) | | |
| — | Shed | 9 50am | MO |
| — | King's Cross | 10 20am | |
| 2 31pm | Leeds Cen | 3 39pm | |
| 5 47pm | Newcastle | 5 53pm | |
| 7 59pm | Edinburgh | — | |
| — | Shed (Fuel and Insp) | | |

Works No 3B diagram next week

### Main line diesel locomotive diagrams
### Gateshead

### Locomotive Diagram GD3A

**Sunday**

| Arrive | Location | Depart | Flag |
|---|---|---|---|
| — | Shed | 11 27am | |
| — | Newcastle | 11 42am | |
| 5 38pm | King's Cross | — | |
| — | Shed (Fuel) | — | |
| — | Shed | — | |
| — | Holloway CLB | 9 20pm | |

**Monday**

| Arrive | Location | Depart | Flag |
|---|---|---|---|
| 1 54am | Newcastle | 1 56am | |
| 4 3am | Edinburgh | — | |
| — | Haymarket Shed (Fuel and Insp) | | |
| — | Haymarket Shed | 7 35am | |
| — | Haymarket Goods Loop | 7 56am | |
| 8 5am | Edinburgh | 8 30am | |
| 10 31am | Newcastle | 10 34am | |
| 2 45pm | King's Cross | — | |
| — | Shed (Fuel) | | |
| — | Shed | 5 5pm | |
| — | King's Cross | 5 35pm | |
| 10 40pm | Newcastle | 10 41pm | |
| 10 51pm | Shed (Fuel and Insp) | | |

Stand Pilot 11 30pm to 7 30am

**Tuesday**

| Arrive | Location | Depart | Flag |
|---|---|---|---|
| — | Shed | 7 35am | |
| — | Newcastle | 7 50am | |
| 12 5pmR | King's Cross | — | |
| — | Shed (Fuel) | | |
| — | Shed | 4 30pm | |
| — | King's Cross | 5 0pm | |
| 9 32pmR | Newcastle | 9 33pm | |
| 9 43pm | Shed (Maintenance) | | |

Stand Pilot 10 30pm to 7 45pm

**Wednesday**

| Arrive | Location | Depart | Flag |
|---|---|---|---|
| — | Shed | 8 5pm | |
| — | Newcastle | 2 20pm | |
| 9 54pm | York | 10 11pm | |

**Thursday**

| Arrive | Location | Depart | Flag |
|---|---|---|---|
| 1 22am | Peterborough | — | |
| 3 0am | King's Cross | — | |
| — | Shed (Fuel and Insp) | | |
| — | Shed | 7 15am | |
| — | King's Cross | 7 45am | |
| 11 3am | Leeds Cen | 12 55pm | |

| Arrive | | Depart |
|---|---|---|
| 4 48pm | King's Cross | — |
| — | Shed | |
| | (Fuel) | |
| — | Shed | |
| | Holloway CLB | 9 20pm |

**Friday**

| | | |
|---|---|---|
| 1 54am | Newcastle | 1 56am |
| 4 3am | Edinburgh | — |
| — | Haymarket Shed | |
| | (Fuel and Insp) | |
| | Haymarket Shed | 7 35am |
| | Haymarket Goods Loop | 7 56am |
| 8 5am | Edinburgh | 8 30am |
| 10 31am | Newcastle | 10 34am |
| 2 45pm | King's Cross | — |
| — | Shed | |
| | (Fuel) | |
| — | Shed | 5 5pm |
| — | King's Cross | 5 35pm |
| 10 40pm | Newcastle | 10 41pm |
| 10 51pm | Shed | |
| | (Fuel and Insp) | |

**Saturday**

| | | |
|---|---|---|
| | Shed | 9 40am |
| — | Newcastle | 9 55am |
| 2 54pm | King's Cross | — |
| — | Shed | |
| | (Fuel) | |
| — | Shed | 7 0pm |
| — | King's Cross | 7 30pm |

**Sunday**

| | | |
|---|---|---|
| 12 44am | Newcastle | 12 54am |
| 3 0am | Edinburgh | — |
| — | Haymarket Shed | |
| | (Fuel and Insp) | |

**Stand Pilot 7 0am to 7 0pm**

| | | |
|---|---|---|
| | Haymarket Shed | 7 25pm |
| — | Edinburgh | 8 5pm |
| 11 5pm | Newcastle | 11 18pm |

**Monday**

| | | |
|---|---|---|
| 1 15am | York | 1 34am |
| 3 42am | Grantham | |
| 6 2am | King's Cross | — |
| — | Shed (Fuel and Insp) | 4 30pm |
| — | King's Cross | 5 0pm |
| 9 32pmR | Newcastle | 9 33pm |
| 9 43pm | Shed (Fuel and Insp) | |

Work No 3B diagram next week

**Main line diesel locomotive diagrams
Gateshead**

**Locomotive Diagram GD3B**

**Monday**

| | | |
|---|---|---|
| | Maintenance | |

**Tuesday**

**Stand Pilot 10 0am to 7 45pm**

| | | |
|---|---|---|
| | Shed | 8 5pm |
| — | Newcastle | 8 20pm |
| 9 54pm | York | 10 11pm |

**Wednesday**

| | | |
|---|---|---|
| 1 22am | Peterborough | — |
| 3 0am | King's Cross | — |
| — | Shed | |
| | (Fuel and Insp) | |
| | Shed | 7 15am |
| — | King's Cross | 7 45am |
| 11 3am | Leeds Cen | 12 55pm |
| 4 48pm | King's Cross | — |
| — | Shed | |
| | (Fuel) | |
| — | Shed | — |
| | Holloway CLB | 9 20pm |

**Thursday**

| | | |
|---|---|---|
| 1 54am | Newcastle | 1 56pm |
| 4 3am | Edinburgh | |
| — | Haymarket Shed | |
| | (Fuel and Insp) | |
| | Haymarket Shed | 7 35am |
| | Haymarket Goods Loop | 7 56am |
| 8 5am | Edinburgh | 8 30am |
| 10 31am | Newcastle | 10 34am |
| 2 45pm | King's Cross | — |
| — | Shed | |
| | (Fuel) | |
| | Shed | 5 5pm |

| Arrive | | Depart |
|---|---|---|
| — | King's Cross | 5 35pm |
| 10 40pm | Newcastle | 10 41pm |
| 10 51pm | Shed | |
| | (Fuel and Insp) | |

**Stand Pilot 10 30pm to 7 30am**

**Friday**

| | | |
|---|---|---|
| — | Shed | 7 35am |
| — | Newcastle | 7 50am |
| 12 5amR | King's Cross | — |
| — | Shed | |
| | (Fuel) | |
| — | Shed | 4 30pm |
| — | King's Cross | 5 0pm |
| 9 32pmR | Newcastle | 9 33pm |
| 9 43pm | Shed | |

**Stand Pilot 10 0pm Fri to 10am Sun**
Works No 3C diagram next week

**Main line diesel locomotive diagrams
Gateshead**

**Locomotive Diagram GD3C**

**Sunday**

| | | |
|---|---|---|
| | Shed | 8 0pm |
| — | Newcastle | 8 15pm |

**Monday**

| | | |
|---|---|---|
| 12 44am | Grantham | |
| 3 6am | King's Cross | — |
| — | Shed | |
| | (Fuel and Insp) | |
| | Shed | 7 15am |
| — | King's Cross | 7 45am |
| 11 3am | Leeds Cen | 12 55pm |
| 4 48pm | King's Cross | — |
| — | Shed | |
| | (Fuel) | |
| — | Shed | — |
| | Holloway CLB | 9 20pm |

**Tuesday**

| | | |
|---|---|---|
| 1 54am | Newcastle | 1 56am |
| 4 3am | Edinburgh | — |
| — | Haymarket Shed | |
| | (Fuel and Insp) | |
| | Haymarket Shed | 7 35am |
| | Haymarket Goods Loop | 7 56am |
| 8 5am | Edinburgh | 8 30am |
| 10 31am | Newcastle | 10 34am |
| 2 45pm | King's Cross | — |
| — | Shed | |
| | (Fuel) | |
| | Shed | 5 5pm |
| — | King's Cross | 5 35pm |
| 10 40pm | Newcastle | 10 41pm |
| 10 51pm | Shed | |
| | (Fuel) | |

**Stand Pilot 11 30pm – 7 30am**

**Wednesday**

| | | |
|---|---|---|
| | Shed | 7 35am |
| — | Newcastle | 7 50am |
| 12 5pmR | King's Cross | — |
| — | Shed | |
| | (Fuel) | |
| | Shed | 4 30pm |
| — | King's Cross | 5 0am |
| 9 32pmR | Newcastle | 9 33pm |
| 9 43pm | Shed | |
| | (Maintenance) | |

**Thursday**

**Stand Pilot 10 30am – 7 45pm**

| | | |
|---|---|---|
| | Shed | 8 5pm |
| — | Newcastle | 8 20pm |
| 9 54pm | York | 10 11pm |

**Friday**

| | | |
|---|---|---|
| 1 22am | Peterborough | — |
| 3 0am | King's Cross | — |
| — | Shed | |
| | (Fuel and Insp) | |
| | Shed | 7 15am |
| — | King's Cross | 7 45am |
| 11 3am | Leeds Cen | 12 55pm |
| 4 48pm | King's Cross | — |
| — | Shed | |
| | (Fuel) | |
| — | Shed | — |
| | Holloway CLB | 9 20pm |

**Saturday**

| Arrive | | Depart |
|---|---|---|
| 1 54am | Newcastle ... ... ... ... ... | 1 56am |
| 4 3am | Edinburgh ... ... ... ... ... | — |
| — | Haymarket Shed ... | |
| | (Fuel and Insp) | |
| | Haymarket Shed ... ... ... ... | 8 20am |
| | Edinburgh ... ... ... ... ... | 9 0am |
| 4 14am | King's Cross ... ... ... ... | — |
| — | Shed | |
| | (Fuel) | |
| | Shed ... ... ... ... ... | 10 0pm |
| | King's Cross ... ... ... ... | 10 30pm |

**Sunday**

| | | |
|---|---|---|
| — | Grantham ... ... ... ... | 12 32am |
| 2 7am | York ... ... ... ... ... | 2 17am |
| 3 49am | Newcastle ... ... ... ... | 3 50am |
| 4 0am | Shed | |
| | (Fuel and Insp) | |

**Stand Pilot 10 0am Sun – 8 0pm Mon**
Work No 3D diagram next week

### Locomotive Diagram GD3D

**Monday**

| | | |
|---|---|---|
| — | Shed ... ... ... ... ... | 8 5pm |
| — | Newcastle ... ... ... ... | 8 20pm |
| 9 54pm | York ... ... ... ... ... | 10 11pm |

**Tuesday**

| | | |
|---|---|---|
| 1 22am | Peterborough ... ... ... | — |
| 3 0am | King's Cross ... ... ... ... | — |
| — | Shed | |
| | (Fuel and Insp) | |
| | Shed ... ... ... ... ... | 7 15am |
| | King's Cross ... ... ... ... | 7 45am |
| 11 3am | Leeds Cen ... ... ... ... | 12 55pm |
| 4 48pm | King's Cross ... ... ... ... | — |
| — | Shed | |
| | (Fuel) | |
| | Shed ... ... ... ... ... | — |
| — | Holloway CLB ... ... ... ... | 9 20pm |

**Wednesday**

| | | |
|---|---|---|
| 1 54am | Newcastle ... ... ... ... | 1 56am |
| 4 3am | Edinburgh ... ... ... ... | — |
| — | Haymarket Shed ... | |
| | (Fuel and Insp) | |
| | Haymarket Shed ... ... ... | 7 35am |
| | Haymarket Goods Loop ... ... | 7 56am |
| 8 5am | Edinburgh ... ... ... ... | 8 30am |
| 10 31am | Newcastle ... ... ... ... | 10 34am |
| 2 45am | King's Cross ... ... ... ... | — |
| — | Shed | |
| | (Fuel) | |
| | Shed ... ... ... ... ... | 5 5pm |
| | King's Cross ... ... ... ... | 5 35pm |
| 10 40pm | Newcastle ... ... ... ... | 10 41pm |
| 10 51pm | Shed | |
| | (Fuel) | |

**Stand Pilot 11 30pm to 7 30am**

**Thursday**

| | | |
|---|---|---|
| | Shed ... ... ... ... ... | 7 35am |
| — | Newcastle ... ... ... ... | 7 50am |
| 12 5pmR | King's Cross ... ... ... ... | — |
| — | Shed | |
| | (Fuel) | |
| | Shed ... ... ... ... ... | 4 30pm |
| | King's Cross ... ... ... ... | 5 0pm |
| 9 32pmR | Newcastle ... ... ... ... | 9 33pm |
| 9 43pm | Shed | |
| | (Maintenance) | |

**Friday**

**Stand Pilot 10 0am to 7 45pm**

| | | |
|---|---|---|
| | Shed ... ... ... ... ... | 8 5pm |
| — | Newcastle ... ... ... ... | 8 20pm |
| 9 54pm | York ... ... ... ... ... | 10 11pm |

**Saturday**

| | | |
|---|---|---|
| 1 22am | Peterborough ... ... ... | — |
| 3 0am | King's Cross ... ... ... ... | — |
| — | Shed | |
| | (Fuel and Insp) | |
| | Shed ... ... ... ... ... | 9 30am |
| | King's Cross ... ... ... ... | 10 0am |
| 2 22pm | Newcastle ... ... ... ... | 2 28pm |
| 4 31pm | Edinburgh ... ... ... ... | — |
| — | Haymarket Shed ... | |
| | (Fuel) | |
| | Haymarket Shed ... ... ... ... | 9 21pm |
| — | Edinburgh ... ... ... ... | 10 1pm |

**Sunday**

| Arrive | | Depart | |
|---|---|---|---|
| 12 9am | Newcastle ... ... ... ... | 12 11am | |
| 5 28am | Holloway CLB ... ... ... ... | — | |
| — | Shed | | |
| | (Fuel and Insp) | | |
| | Shed ... ... ... ... ... | 12 30pm | |
| | King's Cross ... ... ... ... | 1 0pm | |
| 2 50pm | Grantham ... ... ... ... | 2 57pm | |
| 6 43pm | Newcastle ... ... ... ... | 6 44pm | |
| 6 54pm | Shed | | |
| | (Fuel) | | |

Works No 3E diagram next week

### Locomotive Diagram GD3E

| Arrive | | Depart | |
|---|---|---|---|
| — | Shed ... ... ... ... ... | 4 25pm | |
| — | Newcastle ... ... ... ... | 4 55pm | FSX |
| 10 28pm | King's Cross ... ... ... ... | — | |
| — | Shed | | |
| | (Fuel and Insp) | | |
| | Shed ... ... ... ... ... | — | |
| | Holloway CLB ... ... ... ... | 7 51am | MSX |
| 12 46pmR | Newcastle ... ... ... ... | 12 47pm | |
| 12 57pm | Shed | | |
| | (Fuel) | | |
| | Shed ... ... ... ... ... | 4 25pm | |
| — | Newcastle ... ... ... ... | 4 55pm | FO |
| 10 28pm | King's Cross ... ... ... ... | — | |
| — | Shed | | |
| | (Fuel and Insp) | | |
| | Shed ... ... ... ... ... | 12 30pm | |
| — | King's Cross ... ... ... ... | 1 0pm | |
| 4 36pm | York ... ... ... ... ... | 4 42pm | |
| 6 20pm | Newcastle ... ... ... ... | 6 21pm | SO |
| 6 31pm | Shed | | |
| | (Fuel) | | |
| | Shed ... ... ... ... ... | 10 10pm | |
| — | Newcastle ... ... ... ... | 10 25pm | |
| 12 53am | York ... ... ... ... ... | 1 8am | |
| 5 11am | King's Cross ... ... ... ... | — | |
| — | Shed | | |
| | (Fuel and Insp) | | |
| | Shed ... ... ... ... ... | 4 0pm | |
| — | King's Cross ... ... ... ... | 4 30pm | |
| 10 42pmR | Newcastle ... ... ... ... | 10 43pm | |
| 10 53pm | Shed | | |
| | (Maintenance) | | |

Works No 6 diagram next week

### Locomotive Diagram GD3F

| Arrive | | Depart | |
|---|---|---|---|
| — | Shed ... ... ... ... ... | 9 5am | |
| — | Newcastle ... ... ... ... | 9 20am | |
| 1 40pm | King's Cross ... ... ... ... | — | |
| — | Shed | | SX |
| | (Fuel and Insp) | | |
| | Shed ... ... ... ... ... | 2 30pm | |
| — | King's Cross ... ... ... ... | 3 0pm | |
| 7 52pmR | Newcastle ... ... ... ... | 7 53pm | |
| 8 3pm | Shed | | |
| | (Fuel) | | |
| | Shed ... ... ... ... ... | 8 40am | |
| — | Newcastle ... ... ... ... | 8 55am | |
| 2 0pm | King's Cross ... ... ... ... | — | |
| — | Shed | | SO |
| | (Fuel and Insp) | | |
| | Shed ... ... ... ... ... | 5 5pm | |
| — | King's Cross ... ... ... ... | 5 35pm | |
| 11 22pm | Newcastle ... ... ... ... | 11 23pm | |
| 11 33pm | Shed | | |
| | (Maintenance) | | |
| — | Shed | — | |
| — | Gateshead Shed ... ... ... | 10 42pm | SuO |
| — | Newcastle ... ... ... ... | 10 57pm | |
| 12 42am | York ... ... ... ... ... | 12 51am | |
| 3 7am | Peterborough ... ... ... | — | |
| 4 43am | King's Cross ... ... ... ... | — | |
| — | Shed | | MO |
| | (Fuel and Insp) | | |
| | Shed ... ... ... ... ... | — | |
| — | Holloway CLB ... ... ... ... | 7 51am | |
| 12 46pm | Newcastle ... ... ... ... | 12 47pm | |
| 12 57pm | Shed | | |
| | (Fuel) | | |

Works No 5 diagram next week

# 2 List of Locomotives, building and withdrawal dates

| Original No | New No | Date Renumbered (week ending) | English Electric No | Vulcan Foundry No | Date To Service | Date Withdrawn | Original Allocation |
|---|---|---|---|---|---|---|---|
| DELTIC (prototype) | | — | 2007 | Built Dick Kerr Works, Preston | October 1955 | March 1961 | LMR |
| D9000 | 55.022 | 10 April 1974 | 2905 | D557 | 28 February 1961 | 2 January 1982 | HA |
| D9001 | 55.001 | 23 February 1974 | 2906 | D558 | 23 February 1961 | 6 January 1980 | FP |
| D9002 | 55.002 | 8 December 1973 | 2907 | D559 | 9 March 1961 | 2 January 1982 | GD |
| D9003 | 55.003 | 23 February 1974 | 2908 | D560 | 27 March 1961 | 31 December 1980 | FP |
| D9004 | 55.004 | 1 May 1974 | 2909 | D561 | 18 May 1961 | 1 November 1981 | HA |
| D9005 | 55.005 | 2 February 1974 | 2910 | D562 | 25 May 1961 | 8 February 1981 | GD |
| D9006 | 55.006 | 27 March 1974 | 2911 | D563 | 29 June 1961 | 8 February 1981 | HA |
| D9007 | 55.007 | 16 February 1974 | 2912 | D564 | 22 June 1961 | 31 December 1981 | FP |
| D9008 | 55.008 | 9 February 1974 | 2913 | D565 | 7 July 1961 | 31 December 1981 | GD |
| D9009 | 55.009 | 26 January 1974 | 2914 | D566 | 21 July 1961 | 2 January 1982 | FP |
| D9010 | 55.010 | 16 June 1974 | 2915 | D567 | 21 July 1961 | 24 December 1981 | HA |
| D9011 | 55.011 | 16 February 1974 | 2916 | D568 | 24 August 1961 | 8 November 1981 | GD |
| D9012 | 55.012 | 2 February 1974 | 2917 | D569 | 4 September 1961 | 18 May 1981 | FP |
| D9013 | 55.013 | 28 February 1974 | 2918 | D570 | 14 September 1961 | 20 December 1981 | HA |
| D9014 | 55.014 | 2 February 1974 | 2919 | D571 | 29 September 1961 | 22 November 1981 | GD |
| D9015 | 55.015 | 2 February 1974 | 2920 | D572 | 13 October 1961 | 2 January 1982 | FP |
| D9016 | 55.016 | 16 March 1974 | 2921 | D573 | 27 October 1961 | 30 December 1981 | HA |
| D9017 | 55.017 | 9 February 1974 | 2922 | D574 | 9 November 1961 | 31 December 1981 | GD |
| D9018 | 55.018 | 9 February 1974 | 2923 | D575 | 24 November 1961 | 12 October 1981 | FP |
| D9019 | 55.019 | 22 November 1973 | 2924 | D576 | 11 December 1961 | 31 December 1981 | HA |
| D9020 | 55.020 | 10 November 1973 | 2925 | D577 | 12 February 1962 | 6 January 1980 | FP |
| D9021 | 55.021 | 2 January 1974 | 2926 | D578 | 16 March 1962 | 31 December 1981 | HA |

**Abbreviations:**
FP = Finsbury Park (Eastern Region)
GD = Gateshead (North Eastern Region)
HA = Haymarket (Scottish Region)
LMR = London Midland Region

**Notes on allocations:**
The bulk of the fleet, for the majority of its life, remained allocated to the original depots. However, in November 1967 Nos D9001/3/9 went north to Haymarket in exchange for Nos D9000/16/19, to concentrate the air braked examples at Finsbury Park during the conversion programme – they were all "home" again by June the following year.

No D9021 went to Finsbury Park from Haymarket for a seven month period from November 1964.

In May 1979, the Haymarket and Gateshead locomotives were all transferred en block to York. On 1 June 1981, those locomotives on Finsbury Park's allocation not already withdrawn were also transferred to York: ie Nos 55.007/9/15 & 18.

# 3 The Names & Their History

| Original No | Name | Date Named | Where Named | Notes on the name |
|---|---|---|---|---|
| D9000 | *Royal Scots Grey* | 18 June 1962 | Edinburgh | Previously carried by ex LMS 'Royal Scot' No 46101 |
| D9001 | *St Paddy* | 7 July 1961 | Doncaster | Racehorse, bay stallion foaled in 1957. In 1960 won The Derby, St Leger, 2,000 Guineas, Hardwick Stakes and Eclipse Stakes. Owned by Sir Victor Sassoon. |
| D9002 | *The King's Own Yorkshire Light Infantry* | 4 April 1963 | York | Previously carried by ex LNER 'V2' No 60872. However, in that case 'The' was omitted. |
| D9003 | *Meld* | 7 July 1961 | Doncaster | Racehorse, filly foaled in 1952. In 1955 won The Oaks, 1,000 Guineas, Coronation Stakes and St Leger. Owned by Lady Zia Wernher. (Note: of the 'Deltics' named after racehorses, this was the only filly). |
| D9004 | *Queen's Own Highlander* | 23 May 1964 | Inverness | Regimental name not previously used on a locomotive. |
| D9005 | *The Prince Of Wales's Own Regiment of Yorkshire* | 8 October 1963 | York | Regimental name not previously used on a locomotive. |
| D9006 | *The Fife & Forfar Yeomanry* | 5 December 1964 | Cupar | Regimental name not previously used on a locomotive. |
| D9007 | *Pinza* | 22 June 1961 | Doncaster | Racehorse, stallion, foaled in 1950. In 1953 won The Derby. Sire to Pindari, a horse owned by Her Majesty the Queen which came third, in the 1959 St Leger. Owned by Sir Victor Sassoon. |
| D9008 | *The Green Howards* | 30 September 1963 | Darlington | Previously carried by ex LMS 'Royal Scot' No 46133, and ex LNER 'V2' 60835. However, on the 'V2', the letter 'S' on Howards was omitted and the additional legend: 'Alexandra, Princess of Wales' Own Regiment of Yorkshire', was carried. |
| D9009 | *Alycidon* | 21 July 1961 | Doncaster | Racehorse, stallion foaled in 1945. In 1949 won The Ascot Gold Cup, Goodwood Cup, Corporation Stakes and Doncaster Cup. Owned by 17th Earl of Derby. The sire of Meld. |
| D9010 | *The King's Own Scottish Borderer* | 8 May 1965 | Dumfries | Previously carried as 'Scottish Borderer', by ex LMS 'Royal Scot' No 46104. |
| D9011 | *The Royal Northumberland Fusiliers* | 28 May 1963 | Newcastle | Regimental name not previously used on a locomotive. |
| D9012 | *Crepello* | 4 September 1961 | Doncaster | Racehorse, stallion foaled in 1954. In 1957 won The Derby and 2,000 Guineas. Owned by Sir Victor Sassoon. |
| D9013 | *The Black Watch* | 16 January 1963 | Dundee | Previously carried by ex LMS 'Royal Scot' No 46102. However, in that case 'The' was omitted. |
| D9014 | *The Duke of Wellington's Regiment* | 20 October 1963 | Darlington | Previously, as 'The Duke of Wellington's Regt (West Riding)', carried by ex LMS 'Royal Scot' No 46145. |

| Original No | Name | Date Named | Where Named | Notes on the name |
|---|---|---|---|---|
| D9015 | *Tulyar* | 13 October 1961 | Doncaster | Racehorse, stallion foaled in 1949. In 1952 won The Derby, Eclipse Stakes and St Leger. Owned by The Aga Khan. |
| D9016 | *Gordon Highlander* | 28 July 1964 | Aberdeen | Previously carried by ex LNER 'D20' (GNSR Class F) 62277, and ex LMS 'Royal Scot' 46106. |
| D9017 | *The Durham Light Infantry* | 29 October 1963 | Durham | Previously carried by ex LNER 'V2' No 60964. |
| D9018 | *Ballymoss* | 24 November 1961 | Doncaster | Racehorse, stallion, foaled in 1954. In 1957 won The Irish Derby and St Leger and beaten into second place by Crepello in The Derby. In 1958 won Eclipse Stakes and French Prix de L'Triumphe. Owned by Mr S. McShain. |
| D9019 | *Royal Highland Fusilier* | 11 September 1965 | Glasgow Central | Regimental name not previously used on a locomotive. |
| D9020 | *Nimbus* | 12 February 1962 | Doncaster | Racehorse, stallion, foaled in 1946. In 1949 won The Derby and 2,000 Guineas. Owned by Mrs H. A. Glenister. |
| D9021 | *Argyll & Sutherland Highlander* | 29 November 1963 | Stirling | Previously carried by ex LMS 'Royal Scot' No 46107. |

**Notes:**

I   Apart from the 'racehorses', which either had their nameplates fitted from new or during visits to Doncaster Works later, the remainder were named at special ceremonies at the stations quoted. Presumably, it was the time taken to arrange these that delayed the fitting of the plates, and resulted in the namings being spread over several years.

II   Notice how the Finsbury Park (Eastern Region) locomotives were named after racehorses, the Haymarket (Scottish Region) locomotives after Scottish Regiments, and the Gateshead (former North Eastern Region) locomotives after English regiments with north-east connections.

III   All the plates used a 'Clarendon Bold' typeface, Nos D9002/5/8/11/14 & 17 (the Gateshead examples) having plates made of brass and chromium plated, with a slightly smaller size of character. All the other plates were made of aluminium.

IV   Locomotives Nos D9000/4/8/10/13/14/16/19 & 21 were also fitted, at some time in their lives, with regimental badges over the nameplates. However, these were not always fitted at the same time as the nameplates, and had very often been removed before withdrawal.

V   Locomotive No 55.015 carried plaques between the marker lights at each end, commemorating its participation in 'Rocket 150' celebrations at Rainhill in May 1980. These plates were fitted at Finsbury Park 17 March 1981 and state: 'Rocket 150, This Locomotive ran in the Liverpool & Manchester Railway 150th Anniversary Cavalcade at Rainhill 24-25-26 May 1980. This Plaque Presented by the Deltic Preservation Society.'

VI   Locomotive No 55.002 carried plaques over its nameplates commemorating the Friends of the National Railway Museum's involvement in its repaint in the original two-tone green livery. These plaques were unveiled at York Museum during a dedication ceremony on 13 December 1979.

# 4 Main Dimensions: Locomotives & Engines

**Section One: Locomotives**

| | Prototype | Production | | Prototype | Production |
|---|---|---|---|---|---|
| **Length over buffers:** | 67ft 9in | 69ft 6in | **Wheel Diameter:** | 3ft 7in | 3ft 7in |
| **Overall width:** | 8ft 9½in | 8ft 9½in | **Weight in Working Order (ton):** | 106 | 99 |
| **Overall height:** | 12ft 10in | 12ft 10in | | | |
| **Bogie wheelbase:** | 14ft 4in | 13ft 6in | **Maximum axle load (ton):** | 18 | 16.5 |
| **Bogie centres:** | 44ft 0in | 45ft 0in | | | |
| **Total wheelbase:** | 58ft 4in | 58ft 6in | **Continuous tractive effort (lb):** | 29,000 @ 35mph | 30,500 @ 32.5mph |

|  | Prototype | Production |  | Prototype | Production |
|---|---|---|---|---|---|
| Maximum speed (mph): | 90 (later 105) | 105* | Traction motors, type and rating (six per locomotive): | EE 626A – 400bhp @ 533A 600V | EE 913 – 400bhp @ 533A 600V |
| Fuel Tank Capacity (Imp gal): | 800 | 900 (later 826) | Gear ratio, motor to axle: | 61:9 (later 59:21) | 59:21 |
| Water Tank capacity for train heating (Imp gal): | 600 | 640 (later 830) | Train heating boiler type and rating: | Stone Vapor @ 2,000 lb/hr | Spanner Mk 11 @ 2,450 lb/hr |
| Main generator, type & rating (two per locomotive): | EE 831A – 1080 KW | EE 829 – 1089 KW | Total engine bhp: | 3,300 | 3,300 |
|  |  |  | Hp available at rail: | 2,650 | 2,640 |
| Auxiliary generator, type & rating (two per locomotive): | EE 912A – 45KW | EE 913 – 45KW | Full engine output available between: | 18.5 and 100mph | 18.5 and 100mph |
|  |  |  | Minimum Radius curve (without gauge widening): | 4 chains | 4 chains |

* Despite the speed quoted, the locomotives have officially, never been allowed to exceed 100mph in everyday BR service.

**Section Two: Engines**

| Engine type: | Napier D18-25 |
|---|---|
| Description: | Opposed-piston, liquid cooled, two-stroke, compression-ignition engine with a mechanically driven centrifugal scavenge blower. |
| Number of cylinders: | Eighteen |
| Arrangement: | Three banks of three cylinders forming a triangular configuration. |
| Overall dimensions – length= | 93.75in (engine only) |
| length= | 124.875in (with generator) |
| width= | 69.375in |
| height= | 94in |
| Bore: | 5.125in |
| Stroke: | 7.25in × 2 |
| Swept volume: | 5,384cu in |
| Compression ratio – nominal: | 20.7:1 |
| Compression ratio – effective: | 16.2:1 |
| Expansion ratio: | 14.0:1 |
| Rated output – continuous: | 1,650bhp at 1,500 crankshaft speed (rpm) |

| Brake mean effective pressure: | 88.3 (intermittent rating at 1,800bhp) |
|---|---|
| Brake mean effective pressure: | 80.9 (continuous rating at 1,650bhp) |
| Piston speed at 1,500rpm: | 1,812ft/min |
| Scavenge blower type: | Single-state, single-speed, double entry centrifugal with a 15½in diameter impeller and providing 4.2lb/sq in at continuous rating. |
| Net dry weight: | 10,680lb |
| Temperatures – coolant: | 176% F (Outlet at rated output) |
| Temperatures – oil: | 154% F (Inlet at 80lb/sq in) |
| Crankshaft rotation: | 'AB' and 'BC' clockwise, 'CA' anti-clockwise. |
| Output shaft gear ratio: | 0.75:1 |
| Speed, maximum: | 1,125rpm |
| Auxiliary generator and fan drive output: | Up to 200hp at 2,482rpm (Equivalent to 1,500rpm output shaft – 1,125 engine rpm). |

# 5 Preserved 'Deltics'

| Locomotive No | Name | Owner | Current Home |
|---|---|---|---|
| 55.002 (9002) | *The King's Own Yorkshire Light Infantry* | National Collection | National Railway Museum, York |
| 55.009 (9009) | *Alycidon* | Deltic Preservation Society | North Yorkshire Moors Railway, Grosmont |
| 55.015 (9015) | *Tulyar* | Peter Sanson | Mildand Railway Centre, Ripley, Derbyshire |
| 55.016 (9016) | *Gordon Highlander* | Deltic 9000 Fund | Nene Valley Railway, Peterborough |
| 55.019 (9019) | *Royal Highland Fusilier* | Deltic Preservation Society | North Yorkshire Moors Railway, Grosmont |
| 55.002 (9000) | *Royal Scots Grey* | Deltic 9000 Fund | Nene Valley Railway, Peterborough |
| DELTIC (prototype) | *DELTIC* | National Collection | Science Museum, London |

Notes: At the present time (1 January 1985) Nos 55.002, 55.009, 55.019 and 55.022 are in working order, the othters not. No 55.002 is in two-tone green livery, but with full yellow ends and carries both original, and TOPS numbers, so is not strictly correct. The remainder are still in all-over blue, Nos 55.015 and 55.016 in as withdrawn condition, the others repainted. Nos 55.009 has the 'Finsbury Park' white cabs. The prototype is in her original blue with white stripes etc.

# 6 D. Napier & Son Ltd: A Brief History

The old established firm of D. Napier & Son Ltd, has a long and distinguished history and a reputation second to none for its high-power, low-weight, precision-built aero engines. Thus, after branching into the high speed diesel engine market after the last war, they were a natural choice of the Admiralty to commission to develop a high speed and low-weight diesel engine for use in lightweight coastal craft.

Robert Napier (1726–1805) was a Scot born in Levenside, Dumbartonshire, and he became a Blacksmith. To have such skills in those days before the industrial revolution gained momentum, was to be a man of high standing and very much in demand. Robert married Jean Denny – of the famous Clyde shipbuilding family – and they had no less than seven children. One son, another Robert became blacksmith to the Duke of Argyll at Inveraray, and his son David (1790–1873), was the founder of the firm that were later to design the 'Deltic' engine. Incidently, one of Robert's other sons had a son himself, another David and it was this Napier that founded the equally famous Millwall firm of shipbuilders and owners.

The David we are here concerned with lived in Scotland, and it is presumed commenced to serve an apprenticeship in the then infant engineering trade, for in 1808 or thereabouts he went to London to complete his apprenticeship and further his training with Henry Maudslay. Maudslay was of course, one of the fathers of modern engineering. Later David commenced business on his own in York Street, Lambeth, near to where Waterloo Station is now, and on about the site currently occupied by the Royal Festival Hall.

David Napier made his name in engineering circles with the design and construction of printing presses and he gained early fame by interesting the printer of parliamentary papers, T. C. Hansard in his wares. To this day incidently, each day's printed summary of parliamentary proceedings is still known as 'Hansard'.

David had a son, James Murdoch (1823–1895) – known to the family as J. M. – and the business thereafter went under the title D. Napier & Son, J. M. taking an active part as soon as he was old enough. They built up a formidable reputation in the construction of currency coin making and hydraulic machinery as well as cranes, in addition to the printing presses and many other general engineering activities. Expansion of the workshops took place as the industrial revolution got under way and in 1868, as his father's health declined, J. M. become head of the firm.

Unfortuantely, as J. M. himself got older the company's fortunes declined. Only one of his four sons took an active part in the firm and he, whilst being a very sound engineer, did not inherit his father's business acumen. So, when J. M. died in 1895 the firm passed onto the open market and, ironically, was acquired by J. M.'s youngest son, Montague Stanley, from the executors. He had previously taken no part whatsoever in the running of the business.

Montague wasted no time in retrieving the fortunes of the undertaking, moving to larger premises at Acton and, with the business initiative and drive of a fellow called S. E. Edge acting as a selling agent, he diversified into the then expanding private motor car trade. Napiers developed a range of high-powered and high class vehicles for the gentry, of which Edge was able to sell as many as could be produced. Business was so brisk that in August 1906 a private limited company was formed with Montague holding almost the entire share capital. Thus, D. Napier & Son Ltd, was incorporated.

The manufacture of motor cars naturally led to the design and development of their engines and it was in this sphere that the firm excelled. Such was the eventual reputation of their engines that thoughts turned to their use in aeroplanes. At this period of course, flying was comparatively new, but as the war clouds began to loom over Europe the use of aeroplanes as a weapon of war was considered. So Napiers expanded into the aero engine market and, to attract additional capital for yet further expansion, they became a Public Company in 1912.

Many records were being broken by Napier engines and cars, and the firm built up a reputation for high-power and low-weight internal combustion engines for which they became world leaders in the field. Napier engines found their way not only into motor cars and aeroplanes, but also into speedboats so that not only did land and air speed records come their way, but those on the water too. So successful was the entry into the aero engine market that during World War I the firm forsook all other fields, and towards the end of hostilities had developed their famous 'Lion' engine.

The 'Lion' was a magnificent 12-cylinder water-cooled machine packing no less than 450bhp into its weight of just 850lb, and running at 2000rpm. The engine had its cylinders arranged into three banks of four each, and they formed the shape of a broad arrow, with the common crankshaft at the tip. In the 1920s the 'Lion' became the most widely used British built aero engine and apart from a short re-entry into the motor car business in the immediate postwar years, henceforth aero engines became Napiers' lifeblood.

At Montague's death in 1932, a lot of the share capital having passed away from the Napier family, Sir Harold Snagge, a city banker and financier, was elected to the Chair; for the first time in its history the company did not have a Napier at its head. In the years following, much additional capital was raised and other engines developed to replace the ageing 'Lion'. In the same year that Montague died, this engine had reached the state where it was developing 555bhp at 2,350rpm.

The 'Rapier' was the next in the line, originally a sixteen cylinder 300bhp prototype, by June 1934 it was producing no less than 630bhp at 3,500rpm. The cylinders were arranged into four banks, horizontally opposed and with a common crankshaft; a then almost novel arrangement.

By the outbreak of World War 2 Napiers' reputation in their chosen sphere was formidable, their name synonymous with quality. In 1938 another factory was opened at Park Royal, London, and in November the same year, by Government direction and for war production, yet another at Netherton in Liverpool. Production commenced there in early 1940 with a nucleus of staff who had transferred from Acton; by October over 1,000 were employed and it was at this works that the world famous 'Sabre' engine was made. A military use could be found for just about as many of these engines as the company could produce, being a 24-cylinder 2,000bhp unit – one of the world's most powerful piston aero engines of all time.

During the war Napiers took over a whole series of factories, mostly in West London, to make the various component parts by mass production methods, leaving Netherton and Acton actually to assemble the engines. It was during this period that the Government intervened with a scheme that was to lay the foundations of the 'Deltic' locomotive. So important was Napiers' part in the wartime production machine that it was considered they could no longer be trusted with their own destiny. They had built up their reputation on design brilliance and quality but not,

unfortunately for them as it was to turn out, on quantity production, and it was quantity that was needed most at this critical stage in the country's history.

Somebody was needed who could introduce into this old-established and traditional firm 20th century production methods. At that time the English Electric Co Ltd, under the able Chairmanship of Mr (later Sir) George Nelson were one of the country's leaders in the field of mass engineering production, and some of their products were in a similar field to Napiers'. Each and every 'Sabre' engine was needed for the war effort and it was arranged for English Electric to take over the management of Napiers with effect from November 1942. Thus, in December, English Electric acquired the entire equity of Napiers by the simple expedient of exchanging shares of equivalent value on a one for one basis. However, Napiers continued to trade under their own name.

Under the English Electric umbrella Napiers went from strength to strength and after the war thoughts turned to the design and manufacture of turbo-prop, and later jet engines. Napiers' reputation with these being every bit as good as with the piston engines before them. Later the design and development took place of high speed and lightweight – the Napier hallmarks – diesel engines using the two-stroke opposed-piston principle. It was to meet an Admiralty specification that the 'Deltic' engine was developed and, by early 1952 this engine was undergoing service trials.

The actual idea of the Delta cylinder formation of the 'Deltic' engine seems to have originated with the German Junkers 'Jumo' diesel aero engine. This had originally been a 12-cylinder vertical opposed-piston two-stroke with, unlike the Napier 'Sabre', two crankshfts, one at the top of the engine, and one at the bottom. In effect two six-cylinder engines, one on top of the other. The advantages of arranging the cylinders in this fashion, rather than opposite each other and with a single crankshaft, was to obviate the bulky and heavy cylinder heads; in the Junkers arrangement the space between opposing pistons became a common combustion chamber.

Development on these lines goes back before World War 1 and it was found that more weight and bulk was saved in the lack of cylinder heads, than was added by the additional crankshaft and train of gears to combine the two crankshaft outputs. The opposed-piston principle greatly increases efficiency of the cylinders and minimises heat loss; it also allows straight-through (Uniflow) scavenging of the cylinders between power cycles.

Originally Junkers had used a system of connecting rods to connect the upper piston to a single crankshaft at the bottom of the engine, thereby obviating the second crankshaft. However, the use of two crankshafts reduced inertia forces, permitted higher speeds and made a less cumbersome arrangement. Much development work was undertaken on engines following these lines by the Germans between the wars, and by 1939 the 12-cylinder version was developing 1,000bhp at 3,000rpm, being extensively used in aircraft during the war.

Napiers hit on the idea of, in effect, combining three engines on the 'Jumo' principle together but, by using the triangular form, at a cost of only one extra crankshaft – it was a brainwave and the resultant revolutionary, low-weight and fantastically compact power unit, gave high power and a low fuel consumption. Therefore, much weight and space could be saved wherever it was used. Initial installation for test purposes incidently, was in a former German 'E'-boat confiscated after the war.

Production of Deltic engines began in 1953 at Netherton and they soon found their way into fast patrol boats, minesweepers and coastal craft; indeed any vessels with restricted space where high power and low weight were essential. The engines found favour not only with the Royal Navy, but with navies all over the world. Like its 'Lion' and 'Sabre' predecessors, and many other Napier engines that helped to make such names famous as Sir Henry Seagrave, Sir Malcolm Campbell and John Cobb, the 'Deltic' was a record breaker.

In the early 1970s, as a part of a GEC Diesels re-organisation, construction of the 'Deltic' engine was transferred from Netherton to the former Davy Paxman works at Colchester. The engines are still made there, in the main for marine use, by Ruston Paxman Diesels Ltd, a GEC Diesels subsidiary. However, it is perhaps unfortunate that these two old and equally famous names – Ruston and Paxman – are more associated with the heavy oil engine market, than the aero engine from which the 'Deltic' was bred.

# Bibliography

*The Deltics – A Symposium;* C. I. Allen (Editor); Ian Allan 1972, Revised Edition 1977.
*The Deltic Locomotives of British Rail;* Brian Webb; David & Charles, 1982.
*Diesel Impact on British Rail;* R. M. Tufnell; Mechanical Engineering Publications, 1979
*The Eastern Since 1948;* G. Freeman Allen; Ian Allan, 1981.
*English Electric Main Line Diesel Locomotives;* Brian Webb; David & Charles, 1976.
*Men & Machines: A History of D. Napier & Son, Engineers Ltd, 1808–1958;* Charles Wilson & William Reader; Weidenfeld & Nicolson, 1958.
*Power of the 'Deltics';* G. W. Morrison/J. S. Whiteley; Oxford Publishing Co, 1977.
*Profile of the 'Deltics';* G. W. Morrison/J. S. Whiteley; Oxford Publishing Co, 1980.
*Top Shed;* P. N. Townend; Ian Allan, 1975.

*'Deltic Deadline',* journal of Deltic Preservation Society
*Institute of Locomotive Engineers,* journal of
*The Locomotive Railway Carriage & Wagon Review*
*Railway Gazette*
*Railway Magazine*
*Railway World*
*Trains Illustrated/Modern Railways*

Literature, both publicity and technical in respect of the English Electric Co Ltd, and D. Napier & Son Ltd. Both these companies are now a part of GEC Ltd, and their subsidiaries GEC Traction Ltd, and Paxman Diesels Ltd. British Railways technical literature.

# Index